THE MOST IMPORTANT LESSONS IN
ECONOMICS
AND
FINANCE

A Comprehensive Collection of Time-Tested
Principles of Wealth Management

DR. ANTHONY M. CRINITI IV

CRINITI PUBLISHING

D0165660

Published by Criniti Publishing, Philadelphia, PA

ISBN: 0988459523
ISBN 13:   9780988459526

Library of Congress Control Number: 2013946383
Criniti Publishing, Philadelphia, PA

This publication is for informational purposes only. It is sold with the understanding that the author and the publisher are not engaged in providing financial, legal, or other professional services. If financial, legal, or any other form of advice is needed, please consult a financial advisor, an attorney, or another professional advice giving entity.

I would like to dedicate this book to the future heirs of my simple kingdom. This may include the government, which might tax my estate as a source of its revenues. I would also like to dedicate this book to all those who inherit the earth, both present and future. May the lessons taught here be used wisely to improve the world and make it a better place to live and love. Only proper management of money, and other forms of wealth, in the realm of both economics and finance, can lead to the allocation of dedicated, ethical, and great leaders that our world, and all of its beings, deserves.

Table of Contents

Preface

This book was written as a follow-up to my former book, *The Necessity of Finance*, where a foundation was set to explain the characteristics and significance of economics and finance. We now continue our learning journey by exploring the most important lessons of these two sciences. These lessons, expressed in the form of principles, are my bold attempt to summarize what has been learned since the beginning of record keeping on the wealth management of economic and financial entities.

The principles are a result of an accumulation of over fifteen years of notes on these subjects that I have gathered from my experience in the financial field, ranging from being a financial consultant to my current role as a finance professor teaching at the undergraduate and graduate levels at various universities. They are also derived from a variety of sources, including the works of many of the greatest contributors to the two sciences. To my knowledge, they represent the most comprehensive collection of qualitative principles in the field of economics and finance.

I give these lessons to you from the bottom of my heart, with the best intentions, to reveal the secrets of two of the most important sciences. But reading these principles alone is not enough to master them. You must live them. You must think of creative ways to learn these lessons by incorporating them into your daily life. Mastery may take decades, but choosing not to try to master your own wealth can result in harsh consequences, as noted in my previous work.

This book starts with an introductory overview of its contents. Next, there is an overview of various related terminology to help you understand the major concepts used. For example, there is a distinction made between laws, lessons, rules, and principles. Third, there is a chapter on the literature review of the related content. Fourth, there is a chapter that discusses how the categories were created for the actual principles. This book also elaborates on the methodology used and various opportunities for future research. Sixth, a chapter is also dedicated to stating any limitations to the material presented. Next, the weight of this book is in Part 2, where the actual principles are explored. Finally, a conclusion is provided in Part 3 to summarize what was learned in the previous sections of the book.

This book is targeted to a wide audience, particularly beginners to advanced-level economics and finance students. It is recommended that all students read *The Necessity of Finance* before proceeding to this book as it will create a better introduction to the various concepts used. However, it is not required. Beginner students can benefit by exploring the principles individually and building familiarity with various concepts.

Advanced students and practitioners are a particular target for this book. Some of the feedback that I have received from them on my last book is that they wanted a book that can help them improve their wealth. This book is my attempt to capture the most important lessons from the sciences of economics and finance. Learning these lessons better prepares you to manage your wealth to maximize it. Hopefully, these advanced students will be able to capture this knowledge through intense study of these principles.

Economics and finance are very promising sciences that can be helpful to all who spend time studying and practicing it. However, I want to be clear that they are not easy for the average student. This book is designed to be student-friendly, and can be used as a required or supplemental text for colleges or universities. Finally, this book may serve as a direct learning tool to help you create your own path to economic and financial independence.

The information in this book covers a wide variety of topics. Some material may interest you, and some may not. The best way to approach it is with patience. You are encouraged to take notes and review sections that are of interest to you. Later, if you decide to take an economics or finance class, you can always refer back to it for maximum results.

I highly recommend reading this book slowly. If you move too fast, then you may not have reflected deeply enough on the under-lying lessons and/or you may become overwhelmed with informa-tion. In particular, it is recommended that you read no more than five principles a day. Ideally, one principle a day is the best prac-tice. Read it early in the morning when you wake up. Then spend the rest of the day reflecting on the essence of it and how it will help you better understand how to manage your wealth.

Finally, I have attempted to write this book as objectively as possible, but from time to time my opinions may appear. However, this should have a very limited effect on the main goals of the book, which are to expand off the new paradigm of the economic and financial concepts introduced in *The Necessity of Finance*; explore the most important lessons in economics and finance; provide a platform for economic and financial entities to be able to better manage their wealth; and create a foundation for future research studies on these subjects. Enjoy!

PART 1

CHAPTER 1

Introduction

Long before the invention of standardized money, people have contemplated ways to increase their wealth. Unfortunately, only a small minority of people throughout most of modern human history were allowed to enjoy the benefits of being wealthy. Many of the majority lived either as slaves or in deep hopeless poverty; thus, there was little need for them to think about managing something they had little or no right to have. Eventually, many complex events over time have led to many changes in the way humans perceive wealth and the increased probability for anyone to obtain it.

Starting roughly about 250 years ago, it became necessary to create economics, the science of managing wealth for a nation or a division of a nation (here-after called *economic entities*). In the twentieth century, more people obtained more opportunities to become wealthier than any time in history. With the average person advancing in freedom and wealth, around the 1950s it became formally necessary to create finance, the science of managing wealth for an individual, a group, or an organization (here-after called *financial entities*).

Considering the impact that these two sciences have on this world, it is time to step back and review what we have learned. If economics and finance are extremely necessary, as demonstrated in my last book *The Necessity of Finance*, then we need to reflect deeply on their most important lessons. This book has scientific value because it has compiled time-tested principles that provide a better understanding of how to manage wealth for economic and financial entities.

As this book was written in a scientific manner, there are several chapters that the layman reading for fun may want to skip. If you are not interested in how the lessons presented here fit into a scientific paradigm and its methodology, etc., then you may want to go directly now to the actual lessons in Part 2 of this book.

CHAPTER 2

Terminology

Laws

To understand why this book uses principles, we need to clarify some similar terms and explain how they fit into the overall analysis. First, the term "laws" can be ambiguous, as it can refer to natural (also called *universal*) or human-made laws. *Natural laws*, or the laws of nature, are based on the same laws that the natural sciences, such as physics, operate under. These are inherent to all of the forces that act upon us. We did not write these laws; something else did. However, if we can discover them, we can use these laws to our advantage – for example, to make the airplane fly. Contrarily, *human-made laws* were created by humans to help us operate together in society. Examples of this include laws against jay walking or spitting on the sidewalk (currently a law in Singapore).

Rules

Originally, I was tempted to use the term "rules," instead of "principles," when designing this book. But *rules*, generally an unofficial version of human-made laws, have a high probability of being changed, as they are designed to be broken. For example, in one game of cards against a moody card dealer, the rules can change every round. Rules are extremely subjective and can change with the opinion of the ruler. If permanency does exist, it has a limited relationship with rules. Thus, because the word "rules" does not meet the desired objective of coming as close to or equal to having a permanent value, it is, excuse the pun, "ruled out."

This book's principles attempt to reflect natural laws as best as possible, similar to the laws of fire, gravity, and water. That is, I have attempted to ensure that the principles are not human-made. No matter what laws or rules are created by humans, it should not affect the reality of nature's true laws. These laws are more likely to persist regardless of changes to the leaders of various nations and their legal systems. The only way to achieve this goal was to try to restrain my own human limitations and aim for ab-solute objectivity (please see the "Limitations" chapter for more information).

Lessons

How does the term "lesson" fit into our analysis? To keep it simple, a *lesson* **will be defined as some action or thing to learn.** There are many subjects in life with many lessons that you can learn. For example, you can learn a lesson in dancing the tango or flying a kite. **This book is about learning the most important principles in economics and finance.** For the purposes of the book, the most important lessons in economics and finance are also the most important principles in economics and finance. Simply, there is no need to be confused, as the lessons to be learned are in the form of principles.

Principles

There are many who think that principles are eternal. With deep reflection though, it can be realized that humans haven't advanced enough yet to be able to positively state that anything can last forever. *Nevertheless, principles are types of natural laws that are as close to being considered timeless as humanly possible to comprehend.*

Stephen Covey's definition of principles is one of the most useful that I have found and a very helpful start to forming the definition used in this book. He states, "Principles are guidelines for human conduct that are proven to have enduring, permanent value" (Covey, *The 7 Habits of Highly Effective People*, 35). To correspond with the paradigm used in this book, our definition will need some major revisions. Officially, **principles will be defined as natural laws that are indicative to have enduring, highly probable value.** There were several changes made compared to Covey's above definition. First, principles should be more than just guidelines; they need to be natural laws (this was also noted by Covey on the bottom of the same page as quoted above) in order to give them the significance they deserve.

Second, the phrase "for human conduct" was eliminated because a principle is a natural law, which may apply to everything in nature, not just to humans. Third, the word "proven" was replaced by "indicative." As it is very difficult to prove anything in an absolute sense, especially natural laws, the use of indicative allows for more realistic expectations. Finally, for reasons mentioned above, it would be too unrealistic to state that anything has complete permanent value, especially if we are trying to be scientific. How do we know absolutely that anything known to be true today will be true one thousand or even one hundred years from now? It is more helpful to ease up on this part of the definition by substituting "permanent" with "highly probable." The point is that principles will more than likely occur for an extremely long period of time, and possibly to infinity.

The principles in this book were designed to be scientific. To ensure that this is not another book with "maxims" or "words to live by" without any merit, a security system was installed. That is, each principle was subjected to six criteria in addition to the personal scrutiny that I implemented based on many years in the field as a finance professor, a financial planner, a financialist, and an investor. Ideally, I strived for these principles to be highly reliable (or consistent) and highly valid (accurate). Various layers of personal final inspection also were added to ensure objectivity. Also, note that the original list of principles totaled almost a thousand and were accumulated over at least fifteen years of note taking on this subject. Thus, this book is long overdue.

The six major criteria for each principle to be included in this book are listed next. First, each principle needs to be time-tested, which is defined here with an arbitrary range of time of two thousand years minus or plus from the present. In other words, each principle is highly probable that it should have applied two thousand years ago and is highly probable that it should be applied two thousand years from now. Even if the ancients were not aware of or practiced any of these principles, the principles still existed. If they did know about them, then they should have benefited. However, in many cases, it is the current knowledge of the numerous economic and financial mistakes of prior civilizations that have contributed to identifying these principles.

Originally, I was tempted to make the criterion for each principle to be timeless or eternal. But due to the difficulties with claiming anything as permanent, as noted above, using the term time-tested instead allows more flexibility to cope with a realistic time frame and is more practical to current students. Also, because each principle is time-tested with the above defined range of time, it is more measurable and thus more scientific.

The second major criterion for each principle in this book is that it should operate within the framework of economics and/or finance. Each principle has to relate in some way to the overall sciences of economics and/or finance. This criterion was also added to ensure relevancy to the subject matter of this book.

The third major criterion for each principle in this book is that it must be applicable to an economic and/or a financial entity. That is, every principle must apply to a nation or a division of a nation, as in the case of economics, and/or to an individual, a group, or an organization, as in the case of finance. This criterion was added to ensure relevancy to the subject matter of this book.

The fourth major criterion for each principle in this book is that it should lead to wealth maximization for an economic and/or a financial entity. This could happen either directly or indirectly. This criterion was added to ensure relevancy to the primary goals of economics and/or finance, which is to maximize the wealth of their respective entities.

The fifth major criterion for each principle in this book is that it should be highly valid (or accurate) and highly reliable (or consistent). The ultimate goal would be to have always perfectly valid principles or at least have a probability range with six sigma standards. Unfortunately, a limitation of this book is found in the difficulty of scientifically proving the validity of these principles at this point in the absolute sense, due to various constraints like money, space, and time (please see the "Limitations" chapter for more information). This limitation may explain why it is safer to say that these principles are at minimum "generally" true. Despite this limitation, having organized the most important principles in economics and finance with a scientific structure of this sort provides an excellent foundation to future progress in these sciences. It can also act as the bridge connecting what we have learned to what we need to learn more about.

Finally, the sixth major criterion for each principle in this book is that it should be a part of the top 1 percent of all economic and/or financial principles. These elite principles represent the ones that students should learn first. Although inevitably biased (please see the "Limitations" chapter for more information), my selection process was very rigorous and aimed for complete objectivity to meet the goals of this book. When organizing the principles, if I had even the slightest doubt that a principle could not meet the 1 percent test, then it was eliminated. Although this method is not exactly traditionally scientific, as it was based on a subjective rough estimate (out of a hypothetical total of infinite principles), it provided a good starting point. As the total number of principles that exist in the world for these sciences are unknown, there may be many more principles that would also rank in the top 1 percent. Later, future studies may be able to demonstrate better scientifically the validity of these principles as the most important.

CHAPTER 3

Literature Review

This book is the result of the most comprehensive investigation and compilation of the most important principles in economics and finance. Although there are many previous authors who have discussed wealth in various forms, both casually and scholarly, to my knowledge, there is no other work that attempts to scientifically capture the best lessons of wealth management throughout history in the way presented here. Some previous authors have noted important lessons, usually only a few, for various subcategories of the two sciences, for example mutual funds or real estate. Yet these lessons are only a fraction of the two sciences as a whole.

The following is a brief overview of some of the literature that is related to this topic. Although it is certainly not exhaustive, it provides a good starting point to understanding why this book's time has come. Many of the first earliest recorded reflections on wealth dates back to biblical times. There are many little proverbs on wealth found throughout the Old and New Testaments that demonstrates that the ancients had been pondering this topic, at least casually. To keep this analysis more concise, we shall now fast-forward to the era of the great Benjamin Franklin. Franklin's phrases and quotes on wealth, mainly derived from his *Poor Richard's Almanack,* written in the years 1733 to 1758, have been an inspiration for many business-minded people for centuries. His proverbs and statements on wealth represent one of the most extensive collections on this subject up until that point. Thus, it was a major historical reference that I used to frame this work for all economic and financial knowledge pre-Franklin. Although highly entertaining, unfortunately, Franklin's proverbs are random, recognized as unscientific, often overlapping, and generally not often correct when applied to the masses. Furthermore, his work was created before economics and finance were formalized; thus, they were not intended to fit into any scientific paradigm.

The principles of this book are a product of my research mainly from every major economic and financial work starting from Ben Franklin to present. Some of the authors of these works include (listed chronologically), but are far from limited to, Adam Smith, Thomas Robert Malthus, David Ricardo, Karl Marx, John Maynard Keynes, Ludwig von Mises, Friedrich Hayek, John Burr Williams, Benjamin Graham, Harry Markowitz, William Sharpe, and Robert Shiller. Furthermore, I have researched the most important businesspeople throughout the past few centuries, including John D. Rockefeller and Warren Buffett, for some of their own personal lessons. From this research, I have found common themes, consistent with my own experiences in the field, which also have helped shape the principles listed in this book.

In writing this book, I have found that there are several authors who have claimed to list great lessons or rules (or whatever name they chose to help market their book) of "investing" or "business" but generally have not reflected well on the true sciences from which their lessons spring. It appears that the main reason these books were written was for the author's own wealth maximization goals rather than to advance the knowledge in economics or finance. Also, these books usually only arrive at a handful of lessons, most of which can be easily disproved with a little reflection. They are more aligned with my definition of "rules" and hardly close to being considered "principles" as used in this book. Thus, I find it unnecessary for these publications to be mentioned.

In my research, I have found a publication called *The Rules of Wealth* by Richard Templar. At first glance, it appeared like it might be a helpful reference for this book. However, after further inspection, it can barely be considered as having made any striking improvement in the subject.

Contrarily, the following brief list of works deserves the fullest consideration on the subject of enduring lessons on wealth. These publications are listed chronologically by their original publication date followed by the cited page number(s) from the edition listed in the bibliography. Although many contain good lessons, the problem is that they are either random or only applicable to a smaller part of economics and/or finance.

George Clason's *The Richest Man in Babylon* (1926) contains five laws of gold (87) among other similar statements throughout the publication. Napoleon Hill's *Think and Grow Rich* (1937) contains thirteen major principles through which people accumulate fortunes (found throughout various chapters) and thirty major causes of failure (184-191), mainly applicable to the science of financial success, among other similar statements throughout the publication. Henry Hazlitt's *Economics in One Lesson* (1946) contains one major lesson for economics (17). J. Paul Getty's *How To Be Rich* (1965) contains ten rules of business (35-36) among other similar lessons throughout the publication.

Donald Trump's *Trump: The Art of the Deal* (1987) contains several elements of the deal (found in Chapter 2), mainly applicable to real estate investing, among other similar lessons throughout the publication. Stephen Covey's *The 7 Habits of Highly Effective People* (1989) contains seven lessons of personal change, mainly applicable to leadership and management. Dave Ramsey's *Financial Peace Revisited* (1992) contains thirty-seven lessons called peace puppies (282-283), mainly applicable to personal finance, among other similar statements throughout the publication. John C. Bogle's *Bogle on Mutual Funds* (1994) contains twelve pillars of wisdom (302-305), mainly applicable to mutual fund investing, among other similar statements throughout the publication. John Marks Templeton's *Worldwide Laws of Life* (1998) contains two hundred eternal spiritual principles, mainly applicable to investing and life in general. Jack Brennan's *Straight Talk on Investing* (2002) contains ten fundamental principles on investing (213-214), mainly applicable to mutual fund investing, among other similar statements throughout the publication.

Finally, it is important to mention that any literature published prior to my *The Necessity of Finance* in 2013 had a different viewpoint on the sciences of economics and finance. That is, many academic concepts weren't properly framed, specifically the actual definitions of the sciences themselves. Prior to my work, and still to this day, many consider finance a part of economics and have an incomplete perception of how the sciences interrelate. Thus, prior works were limited because their authors were not fully able to investigate and discover true principles of wealth management without this proper framework. I stress, it is only an accurate understanding of the paradigm created from *The Necessity of Finance* that could have helped to clearly assemble the principles arrived at in this work.

CHAPTER 4

About Categories Devised

To organize the book better and to create a more reader-friendly experience, the principles were grouped into various related categories. The categories that were created include some of the most popular subjects that are related to economics and finance, such as business (includes corporate finance and various forms of business management), charity, debt, diversification, economics, ethics, financial psychology, health, human resources (this includes hiring and firing of employees and general management), international finance, investing, marketing, money, personal finance, planning, and saving. The principles that did not fit properly into the above categories were moved into the general economics and finance miscellaneous category.

As personal finance is a very unique subscience of finance that deserves special attention, many subcategories were created for this subject including: education, employment, estate planning, family and friends, habits, personal assets, retirement, shopping, and wealthy people. The principles that did not fit properly into the above categories were moved into the personal finance miscellaneous category.

There were many other possible related economic and financial topics that were considered in being classified as a category. However, these subjects either overlapped with existing categories or were better addressed in a miscellaneous section. Nevertheless, these subjects were considered, either directly or indirectly, in the formation of the total list of principles. For your convenience, the following is an abbreviated list of these miscellaneous subjects: accounting, agricultural and natural resource economics, capital, economic finance, environmental and ecological economics, financial economics, government price fixing, health insurance, imports and exports, inflation, insurance, international economics, labor and demographic economics, leadership, macroeconomics, markets, microeconomics, minimum wages, monetary and fiscal policy, national debt, population control, public economics, rent control, risk management (includes insurance), sales, statistics, tariffs, taxes, trade embargos, unemployment, union wages, and urban economics.

In short, the most important principles in economics and finance were derived after carefully considering all of the most important related subjects and their respective lessons.

CHAPTER 5

Methodology and Future Research

The principles of the book were created mainly using personal qualitative analysis methods. In particular, they were created from my many years of field experience, including but not limited to my work as a finance professor, a financial planner, a financialist, and an investor. The principles were gathered from at least fifteen years of observations and note taking in the financial field. The original list of total potential principles that was accumulated amounted to more than one thousand. However, this list was significantly reduced in order to meet the high standards of an ideal true principle defined earlier.

Many of the principles in this book were also derived from past qualitative as well as quantitative analysis done by other economists, financialists, and economic and financial managers, both directly and indirectly. For example, the benefits of diversification have been demonstrated numerically by many of the original founders of finance, including Harry Markowitz and William Sharpe. In practice, the benefits of diversification have also been demonstrated through the effects of a mutual fund on a financial entity's portfolio.

Although very little quantitative analysis was done directly by the author to form the principles in this book, the principles were structured methodically to eventually overcome this limitation. That is, each principle was structured for future survey research and data analysis. Surveys are known to represent quantitative research. They generally also come with the disadvantage of having low validity but with the advantage of having high reliability. The principles could be incorporated into various types of questionnaires, particularly Likert scale style, in order to further demonstrate the credibility of each one. Future survey research could complement the qualitative field research already used, in addition to the possible use of other scientific methods like case studies or experiments, in order to increase the overall validity of these principles.

In Appendixes A and B, two Likert scale questionnaire samples (Questionnaire Sample A and Questionnaire Sample B, respectively) were created as a guideline for future studies. For convenience reasons, it was much easier to display a sample of the first ten principles in this book in each questionnaire instead of them all. It is recommended that anyone who completes these questionnaires, or any similar future questionnaires, should read this book in its entirety first in order to enhance their validity. By reading this book, respondents may be more equipped to understand the principles. This in turn may help to eliminate the ambiguity often associated with surveys.

The Likert scale sample questionnaires have five mutually exclusive choices for each principle: strongly agree, agree, neutral, disagree, and strongly disagree. The first sample attempts to determine the respondent's overall opinion of the validity of each principle. The second sample attempts to determine the respondent's opinion on whether each principle should be listed as one of the most important lessons in economics and/or finance. Remember that these two short samples are for illustration purposes only. There are a variety of other creative ways to present these principles in survey form to help measure their significance to their respective sciences. Also, there are many other considerations that help to add credibility to any survey, including the sampling procedure and the data analysis methods used.

CHAPTER 6

Limitations

There are several limitations to consider from the material presented in this book. First, there are so many important lessons to learn from economics and finance that it was very difficult to determine specifically which ones are the most significant. The selection of the principles is based on the author's opinion from personal experience. The principles were included that I thought would be approximately a part of the top 1 percent of all economic and/or financial principles. The rest were discarded. Although, this method is not exactly traditionally scientific, it provided a good starting point. Later, future studies may be able to demonstrate better scientifically the validity of these principles as the most important.

A second limitation of this book is found in the difficulty of scientifically proving the validity of this book's principles in the absolute sense. Some may argue that this is an unnecessary point, as it may be impossible to prove anything in an absolute sense. Nevertheless, to be thorough, this limitation is acknowledged. Although rare exceptions may exist, conservatively speaking, at minimum these principles are "generally" true. As noted already, future studies may help to enhance the validity of each principle.

A third limitation of this book is that it is written by a financialist, although it incorporates lessons from both economics and finance. Although I tried to be objective, it is possible that my opinions as a financial scientist may have had a biased effect on the quality of the economic principles. Optimistically, this limitation may have a positive effect by allowing economists to revisit their subject from an alternative perspective.

Fourth, very little quantitative analysis was used by the author to form the principles in this book. However, the principles were structured methodically to eventually overcome this limitation by allowing for future survey research and numerical data analysis. Please review the "Methodology and Future Research" chapter for more information.

Fifth, it is extremely difficult to accurately calculate the probability of the principles listed here to be applicable within the designated arbitrary range of time of two thousand years minus or plus from the present. Thus, I was forced to generalize their applicability based on my knowledge of major economic, financial, and historical events of the many existing civilizations during the past two thousand years. I then used these generalizations to forecast their general applicability in the next two thousand years. Also, considering the limited amount of historical data available, its high probability for being biased, and the unknown element of predicting future events, this book forces us to revisit our preconceived idea of what eternity is. Although there are many examples of authors who claim to offer eternal principles or rules (or whatever name they choose to call it) for various subjects, the research for this book demonstrates that it is difficult enough to show that a principle is time-tested even when a range of time has been specified, and at the moment, it is impossible to show that it is timeless.

Sixth, this book is limited in that it is a human's attempt to capture the natural laws in economics or finance. These natural laws, by definition, were created by a force or forces beyond our current comprehension. There is a possibility that our human limitations (for example, physical or psychological) may impede us from ever completely revealing the natural laws of any science. Despite these limitations, it should not deter us from trying.

Seventh, each of the principles is analyzed very briefly. Due to the extent of the scope of this book, it would be impossible to give a full analysis of each principle and maintain a reasonable length. For example, some principles probably would take volumes of texts to fully analyze their significance but may have been reduced to several sentences for the reader's convenience.

Eighth, these principles may overlap with each other in various degrees. I have tried very hard to ensure that every principle is entirely unique. However, at some point, all of these principles interrelate within their respective sciences.

Finally, this book is limited because it is not complete. That is, it is a work in progress. The complete list of the most important lessons in economics and finance may never be acquired until all of the knowledge from both of these sciences is obtained. Although this event may be very distant, we should not let this deter us from enjoying the benefits of this book.

It is hoped that you can consider the difficulties in writing a book of this magnitude in order to excuse the limitations listed above (and any others not mentioned). Unfortunately, limited resources, such as money, space, and time, impeded this current study from gathering more quantitative supporting data. Despite these limitations, this book teaches many better ways to manage wealth formed mainly from an often underappreciated qualitative methodology, which includes many years of a variety of my experiences in the financial world. In addition, I have also spent many years researching many of the greatest minds in the fields of economics and finance to gather ideas for this book.

Now, I would like to introduce to you the most important lessons (in the form of principles) in two of the most important sciences to our planet. It is hoped that you will treasure them all!

PART 2

CHAPTER 7

The Most Important Principles in Economics and Finance

Business

Principle 1

---

*It can take a lifetime to build a solid business
and moments to destroy it.*

A person can work forty years building a business and then suddenly make a bad decision that jeopardizes everything. Examples include taking out a bad loan, buying too much inventory of the wrong product, unethical behavior, and mistreating customers. It is essential for business owners to understand that all of their actions can have significant positive or negative reactions. Every major decision that could impact a business should be thought through fully before it is implemented. If the decision requires a specialist like an attorney, then that option should also be carefully considered.

Principle 2

It is the owner's responsibility to ensure that her or his business survives, not the customer.

An owner's business failure will generally have a bigger impact on the owner's wealth rather than the customer's. Thus, it is the owners who need to ensure that the products or services that they sell are what the customer wants. Feedback from the customer is crucial to determining what changes need to be made to a business, if any. When customers give feedback, as bad as it may be, the owners should be thankful because they are giving you information that they are not obligated to give you.

As hard as it may be to take constructive criticism from the customer when offered, you must take this information very seriously as it may contain strong truths to help your business grow (or avoid insolvency). Many times costumers will not tell you why your business is failing and what is impeding them from buying your products or services (or more of them). Then you should reward costumers to give you their opinion (maybe via surveys). This information is vital to every business. Alternatively, an owner can put herself or himself in the customer's shoes and try to look at the business from the other perspective. This can be extremely effective, especially through undercover visits to the business locations. To solve your business problems, you must sometimes think like your customers to find your flaws.

Principle 3

Many singles may be better than one home run.

This principle is explained in terms of the sport of baseball, where one home run equals the same point as four consecutive singles. A first-time player to the sport may easily conclude that it is better to consistently aim for home runs every time instead of singles. The problem with this logic is that it doesn't consider the difficulty in hitting a home run consistently as compared to a single. This baseball analogy is similar to a business.

Consider a rare business that has only one client, for example, an attorney whose only client is a billionaire. Most attorneys would agree that to have this rare situation is like hitting the lottery. However, it is much more probable for the average attorney to be financially successful by taking on many smaller clients. This client-accumulation process is much more reliable. In addition, consider the effect of the loss of income if the attorney above lost his only client. He will now have no money coming in. On the other hand, if an attorney with one thousand clients lost one client, then he may not even feel it.

Principle 4

Almost every idea can transform into a successful business if applied correctly.

Ideas (and start-up costs) are the foundation to any business. They usually come from random gatherings with family or friends while discussing brilliant ways to make a living. Many typical businesses fail because the lessons in finance were not considered before the idea was implemented. Yet there are many examples of successful businesses that are atypical. Some examples include a baby-hair weave company, a mob museum, or a murder-scene cleanup company. The inventive process must be coupled with a realistic financial plan and the desire to make it happen.

Principle 5

An army of many can't stop an idea whose time has come.

The natural ability to recognize and capitalize on an idea new to the world can be invaluable. It may take years of failure and hard work to give you the skills to identify an opportunity that may only come once in a lifetime. Those who have made valuable discoveries should ensure that they have as much legal protection as the law allows before making it public. **Everything you have worked for your whole life may come down to one moment to become a financial success.** When this situation occurs, "carpe diem" (seize the day).

Principle 6

Never let your competitors know what you're
thinking before your ideas are publicized.

Capitalize on your ideas before announcing them. With your secrets revealed, the competition may redirect money that could have flowed to you. By telling your ideas to the world ahead of time, you are allowing others to process that idea and determine whether they want a piece of the pie. Even if you have legal rights to a certain idea, preliminary announcements may awaken sleepy giant competitors, who will do anything in their power to ensure that you will have to share your profits. It is much better to keep your thoughts to yourself until you have thoroughly researched and implemented your plan. At the point where information becomes public, you will have to shift gears to the accelerated profit-maximization phase (see next principle).

Principle 7

When making more money than the competition because of a rare advantage, it is time to work harder than ever.

When those rare opportunities present themselves and give you an advantage for consistent profits when everyone else can't figure out what you're doing right, then you need to accelerate your work even faster. Take every ounce that is due to you and strengthen your position before the competition figures out your strategy and replicates it (and competitors always will). These opportunities are extremely rare and must be capitalized on completely. It's like playing musical chairs and only you know exactly how long the song is. When the music is over, you better have the best seat or else you may have wasted the greatest opportunity of your lifetime.

Principle 8

Knowledge breeds wealth.

Continuously invest in the knowledge of your trade and mastering the concepts of finance. This strategy will pay good long-term dividends. The best of any occupation always command, and generally receive, a higher premium for their superior skills. It takes time and knowledge to obtain those skills and keep them sharp. Even when you reach the top, you must continuously learn more to maintain your status.

This also applies to finding better ways to instruct your employees to perform their job better. If your employees are the smartest in your field, everything else being equal, then your organization should dominate the competition.

Principle 9

*If you have the option, eliminate the difficult clients
for maximum efficiency.*

In every business, there will always be difficult clients. These are the clients who take up 90 percent of your time and may only contribute about 10 percent to your income. The same clients are usually the ones that make you want to quit your business as they hand you the most stress. Consider the effect that it would have on your schedule and your ability to generate more income by eliminating these clients (if you have the option). You now will be able to spend more time on finding easier clients who require less time and energy. The result could be more income and time, less income risk as you have now increased your total clients (as your number of clients increase, the loss of one client will generally affect your income less because there are many more clients still left), and less stress.

Principle 10

*If you have the option, choose your customers
based on their character and not their wallet size.*

A client or customer may appear to bring great wealth to your business, but underneath he or she may be an accident waiting to happen. The liabilities that may follow with such a client may overbear all potential gains. For example, a fight promoter may take on a new wealthy client who has the potential to be a great professional fighter. This client can bring a significant amount of income to the business. However, the promoter may be aware that this client is also mentally unstable, a trouble maker, and is constantly getting into legal issues.

If the client happens to get into trouble with the law, then the promoter's whole business may become wide open to lawsuits. This client may be more trouble than he or she is worth. By avoiding these types of clients, although they may be very tempting, the total risk of the business is decreased and its long-term stability is increased.

Principle 11

The mixture of business and family is a potential time bomb.

There are certain situations where family members do work well together for long periods of time. This usually occurs when their business and personal goals are aligned and their personalities are very compatible. However, this situation is very rare.

Particularly when financially pressed, it is usually better to avoid the temptation to involve family with your business affairs. It takes an in-depth knowledge of the inner workings of finance and the proper business mentality to succeed in business. This is a very rare quality that becomes even rarer when trying to find more than one family member with these same qualities. Thus, in a family business, generally there is at least one family member who in isolation does not stand a chance at being a business success. The manner that he or she conducts business affairs may inevitably conflict with the other family member(s) who are more business-minded. The unavoidable conclusion may take years to come to fruition, but when it does, it may result in irreparable damage to relationships with the people that you love the most. You have to ask yourself, "Is it worth the risk?"

Principle 12

Studying your competition strengthens your position.

Know your enemy's strengths and weaknesses to capitalize on opportunities. You should know your competitors well enough to know what advantages and disadvantages they have compared to you. You may want to start your research with a SWOT analysis (strengths, weaknesses, opportunities, and threats) of your industry first. Then narrow your focus to each individual competitor one at a time. When you know your competitors well, then you will be able to know how to react to their every move. You will become better at predicting the consequences of their moves, and your possible reactions, to continuously position your business at a favorable advantage.

Principle 13

Businesses must keep the customer happy at every encounter.

Every negative event with a customer increasingly lowers the probability of the maximum sale and/or tip that one may have earned. From the time that a customer enters the door until the moment that he or she leaves, the maximum amount of money that the customer is willing to give may be progressively reduced from every event that is perceived as unfavorable to that customer. For example, let's pretend a family goes to a restaurant to have dinner. When they walk in, it takes an hour just to get seated. Psychologically, this family is already building up a savings of dissatisfaction that will result in a lower tip or lost future sales (by never coming back again). Then when they sit down the waiter appears to rush them through the meal. Another deposit to the dissatisfaction account. Finally, their young child is unapologetically hit by the waiter as he is passing through the isle. Final strike.

Do you think this family is coming back here to eat again? Probably not. Do you think the waiter received a good tip? He is lucky if he received anything. After all, a tip is a reflection of the satisfaction level of the customer. All of this could have been avoided if the business was on its toes the whole time ensuring the customers were satisfied during their whole stay.

Principle 14

*Every encounter with a customer is an opportunity
to increase profits.*

You should strive to make at least one sale from every customer or client who walks into your place of business. The most successful business-people know that the hardest part of sales is to get people into your doors. Once they're inside, generally there are three major reasons why they will walk out without buying anything. First, they don't have enough money. Second, you have products or services that they don't want or need. Third, your salespeople failed to do their job. If potential customers have walked into someone's business, their action has already showed interest. If they have the money and they are interested in your products or services, then it is up to the sales team to close the sale.

For example, a great clothing salesperson could sell several hundred dollars' worth of clothes to a person who only came into the store to buy a belt or a pair of shoes. The salesperson may have showed the customer all new clothing lines and spent the time ensuring that they matched the customer's wants. The salesperson opened up opportunities for more sales by cross-selling other products or services that the customer may not have immediately registered that he or she needed. The longer the customer was in the store being satisfied, the more unanticipated sales that were generated.

Principle 15

Customers love cheap prices but despise cheap business owners.

To be business-savvy with your customers is smart business. However, to be cheap and petty with customers is highly insulting, particularly with insignificant items, and is only a product of short-term thinking. This can cost you future sales and generate a bad reputation. Customers generally despise cheap business owners and will go out of their way to tell everyone they know about their bad experiences.

In business, it is important to give a little to your customers if it will translate to more profits in the future. For example, loss leaders are a very effective strategy. Here you may sell a product or service and make a little (or no) profit. However, you may make the customers happy that they got a good deal, and they will more than likely come back for more business. Some other examples of good business tactics include little things like giving a free drink for loyal restaurant customers every now and then or taking a little off a good tenant's rent for the holidays. These may appear insignificant events to you but are flattering to the customer and can have long-lasting unexpected positive effects on your wealth. For a small price you may have bought yourself lifelong customers or clients.

Principle 16

Buy low and sell high, yet lower than your direct competitors.

To make a profit, a business must sell its products or services above their costs (unless the business is implementing a loss-leader strategy, etc.). The lower you pay for your products and services, the more you can make. Also, the higher the price that you can sell your products and services, the more you can make. The catch to the last statement is that you must not sell too high to chase the customers away. Generally, you should strive to sell high yet lower than your competitors (unless your product or service is superior in quality). If you only make a little profit on every transaction but sell a lot more because of your lower price, then you may bring in a larger total profit. This is another common sense principle that is often neglected and probably a major reason for most business failures.

Principle 17

Sacrifice some if necessary for the survival of the whole.

When preparing for rough times (or in the midst of it), you need to find and eliminate the unnecessary aspects of your wealth (i.e., expenses or unproductive assets) in order to ensure survival. This will allow more energy to be focused truly on what financial resources will increase the bottom line. This is similar to a tree that sheds its leaves for the winter to be able to reallocate more of its energy internally and protect its roots. This will help it to concentrate on defending its core assets and surviving the hard cold weather.

If you know that extremely difficult financial times are on the horizon, then that is when it is time to do the most soul-searching to determine what you really need and what can be eliminated. For example, at the personal level, assets that may be discarded include the yacht, the extra car, the bigger house, and any expensive clothing. For a business, assets that may be discarded include the bigger headquarters, the executive jets or limos, or the overpaid and underproductive executives. This may not be fun, but it certainly may be the deciding factor for surviving hard economic and/or financial times.

Principle 18

Simplifying your product or service has strong marketing appeal.

There is a tipping point to providing options for your customers or clients. Some options may be enticing; however, too many options will generally repel customers. The more layers of options that you add, the more likely that you may not get the sale. You may end up losing the customers' interest after the first few seconds if they don't understand what it is that they are buying.

Restaurants are perfect examples. Many of the most successful restaurants have the simplest menus (usually just a one-page lunch or dinner menu). Restaurants that offer their customers several menu books have made their customers work harder and provided a disservice. There are some products that are naturally complicated and test this principle. However, even the most complicated products, such as cars and computers, are sold more when the customers' user-friendliness is maximized. Simple sells.

Principle 19

*Being clear about your expectations to employees
will help you to maximize their efficiency and loyalty.*

If your laborers do not understand their job completely, then this will cost you money. Unnecessary work will have been completed, you will be frustrated, and your workers will be angry that their work was not appreciated. Generally, if the expectations of a task are clear and the job is performed improperly, then it is the fault of the employee. If the expectations of a task are not clear and the job is performed improperly, then it is the fault of the employer.

This principle is as true in business as it is in the military. A general's responsibility entails giving his soldiers unquestionably clear orders for them to complete their mission. A general's ambiguous instructions can cost his soldiers their lives. Similarly, a business owner's ambiguous instructions can cost her employees their livelihood.

Principle 20

Give business to those who give business to you.

You may not be able to use this principle 100 percent of the time, as it may sometimes be impractical. However, in general, by sending business back to people who have given you business, you can send a valuable message that you care about them. Subconsciously, this message is processed with long-lasting positive effects on your business relationship. They may send you a wave of referrals never imagined.

This rule becomes more appropriate when the person can have a big effect on your wealth. For example, you may want to use and/or refer the tax services of an accountant who happens to be one of your biggest customers. This can lead to new and prosperous business opportunities for both parties.

Principle 21

Always keeping your promises can help you to keep your good reputation.

If you give someone your word, then you must fulfill it. If you say that you are going to meet someone at a certain time, then don't be late (or call if you are going to be). If you say that you will lend someone money for an investment project, then lend it. Any successful businessperson whom you may associate with will automatically devalue the worth of your reputation if you don't do what you say you are going to. This may result in serious long-term consequences, including forcing you only to be able to do business with other disreputable business-people. Honorable business-people generally only work with others like themselves and may not allow you back into their circle of influence.

There may come a time where it is impractical to keep a promise if an unexpected situation has changed the course of events – for example, a robbery causes you to be shy of loan payments. It is your responsibility to work with the person or people that you made a promise to until the situation is resolved (even if it takes years). Ignoring the problem only ruins your reputation and makes the situation worse.

Principle 22

The primary goal of any business should be to maximize the owner's wealth.

Businesses are created to make the owners rich. They may have other secondary goals, in particular to maximize profits from the sale of goods or services, but their main concern should be to expand their wealth. If their main goal was to maximize wealth for the benefit of a specific cause other than the owner, then they are not businesses but charities. For a complete discussion of this difference, please review Chapter 19: Finance and Business from *The Necessity of Finance*.

Many times businesses, whether corporations, partnerships, or sole proprietors, forget why they are in business (as hard as that is to believe). When this occurs, they start to conduct activities that are contrary to their goals, such as giving away too many products or services for free. This is the start of many financial problems.

Principle 23

Businesses can maximize their revenue if they focus on understanding what other people want and not only what they want.

Dale Carnegie said it well: "Every act you have ever performed since the day you were born was performed because you wanted something" (Carnegie, *How to Win Friends and Influence People*, 34). In the complicated form, even your kindest actions, such as giving, was done because you wanted something in return. In that case, it may have been just a feeling that you made somebody happy. However, most situations are easier to demonstrate, particularly, in business. Customers generally always look for a product or service that matches their needs and wants.

Customers don't like to be sold things unless they help resolve their problems. They also don't like a pushy salesperson whose eyes glow with the profits he or she can make from the sale. If you treat customers with a good heart and listen to what they really want, then they will go out of their way to help your business succeed.

Principle 24

A business should only move at the speed at which it is prepared to handle.

If a business takes on more clients or customers than it is capable of managing, then it risks losing significant revenues. Competition will be created much sooner as the knowledge spreads of the business's inability to match its supply with the demand. An unprepared business also angers customers by wasting their time. For example, a short-staffed firm may make their customers wait hours for products or services that it is unprepared to deliver. More employees may have rectified the situation. However, the company also may not have the proper infrastructure to deal with all the new sales (e.g., the office is too small or there is not enough required machinery).

Slow and steady generally wins the business race. If you can build a business in small pieces, then that gives you enough time to learn how to grow your type of business. There is a learning curve to every business. If you maximize your sales demand while you are still at the bottom of the curve, then you risk being unable to properly manage a high sales volume. Many angry customers can quickly result in no customers.

Principle 25

Quicker wise actions avoid costly reactions and create profitable transactions.

When confronted with a good business decision that you believe in, where competitors can equally capitalize on the same information, then it is important to implement this decision before anyone else can process the implications. For example, let's say that you have knowledge of a stock that has great earning potential at the right price. Even though this knowledge is public, there may not be many big investors who have capitalized on this opportunity yet. Let's pretend that many of the biggest potential investors were all out together that day playing golf with no access to the market. If you were to buy the stock before substantial amounts of investors did (including all of these golfer investors), then you have the potential to make more money than they do.

In this case, you have discovered and implemented a good business decision before anyone has figured it out. Other investors will have to react to your good decision probably at a higher cost. When these situations occur, although they are rare, one is in a great position to quickly enhance wealth. To be successful in business, you must master the art of quick decision making. The quicker one can make a good business decision, the higher the odds of one's success over their competitors.

Principle 26

The greater they are, the harder they failed.

Many great initial failures are common characteristics of the most successful business-people and investors. The same is true for great people from all fields, including leaders in the military, most natural sciences, and politics. Thomas Edison, the world's most famous inventor and also a great businessman, treasured failure because he recognized, like other greats, that it was an opportunity for growth if you can learn from it. His invention of the lightbulb was only made possible after thousands of failed attempts.

Persistency is a necessary quality of every successful business-person. It's not so much about failing but how you overcome it. We all must fail at something at some time, and failure should not be a reason for giving up. It is the one who learns most from failure and keeps on going that capitalizes best.

Principle 27

The more products or services that are bought, the lower your costs could be.

The ability to buy in bulk is an advantage for businesses to negotiate a lower price. If you have the opportunity to buy in large quantities, then you generally have the upper hand in directing the cost. A supplier of bricks, for example, may charge a random customer full retail value for a small trunk-load of bricks. However, a customer who owns a large construction company that will require many bricks is a completely different customer. This customer has the ability to bring a high volume of business to this supplier. This fact puts the larger-sized customer in a higher position of negotiating. If that customer is given a discount, then he or she may give the supplier his or her business. Out of fear of loss of many potential future sales, suppliers will generally make exceptions that they would not do for the smaller customer. This principle can also apply to consumers and investors.

Charity

Principle 28

A true gift is unconditional.

People can be controlled to a degree by money and other forms of wealth. When you give a true gift to someone, a group, or an organization, you have to be prepared to let go of it and the control factor that may be attached. Real charity means to give something, including money, because you mean it from the bottom of your heart. Thus, the recipient of the gift should be allowed to enjoy 100 percent of the gift without feeling obligated to pay back. If the recipient has to pay it back, then the gift is a loan in disguise.

Principle 29

Only give gifts that you can afford to give.

As the great investor Donald Trump said, "It's easy to be generous when you've got a lot, and anyone who does, should be" (Trump, *Trump: The Art of the Deal*, 367). Rich people can give millions (even billions) of dollars away a year and never lose an ounce of sleep. To them, it could be just a portion of the annual interest due to them. Philanthropy can make wealthy people look good and generate a lot of publicity. In the end, the free publicity may translate into a replacement of the original gift with more revenue to their businesses. Based on these statements, was this really a gift or funds allocated to an incognito advertisement fund? As Trump also mentions on the same page as the above comment, for similar reasons just stated, it generally means more if wealthy people give their time.

It is much harder to be generous with your money when you are not wealthy. A middle-class blue-collar worker may barely be able to give 5 to 10 percent of her or his income to various charities. A poor person may not have a nickel to give after the bills are paid every month. How can such a person be expected to give money to charity? Large charitable gifts by those who can't afford it may worsen their situation. But just like the wealthy person, money is not the only thing that you can give. A poor person can also give her or his time to helping someone, for example, by walking an older person's dog or cleaning up the streets for the neighborhood. We all can make a difference regardless of our current financial status.

Debt

Principle 30

Always paying your debts allows you to be repaid
with credibility.

When you borrow money from someone, you should always pay it back. This especially applies to family and friends as they are your lifeline in emergency situations. If you don't pay your debts, then you lose credibility. This means that people won't believe in your promises any more (the origin of the word *credit* comes from the Italian word *credere,* which means *to believe*). It is very difficult to survive in our modern civilization coasting by on minimal levels of society's trust.

Principle 31

There are legitimate reasons for taking out a loan.

Borrowing money is sensible if used properly. For example, a business start-up loan can put a hard worker in business. The money that the borrower may generate from the loan may pay itself back thousands of times in her life. Yet without that initial loan, she may never have had the chance to make it happen. Of course, it is important to ensure that you only take out what is needed and can be paid back (see next principle).

Principle 32

You should borrow only what you can afford to pay back.

This principle hardly needs an explanation, yet it never fails to cause serious financial consequences. This lesson may have prevented the current Great Recession and plenty of other similar events. Any economic or financial entity that borrows money must eventually pay it back. There is a tipping point of excessive debt that is unique to everyone. It is your responsibility to study your financial status and determine what that number is. To find it, you will need to explore your income status and your real reasons for wanting more debt. If you borrow too much, then the interest on the debt may eat you alive.

Principle 33

It is your responsibility to collect money that is owed to you.

Be persistent to capture debt owed to you. When dealing with people who are trying to get over on you, then take no bad excuse as hostage. The deadbeats will play their game, but you must be prepared to counter them. Find creative ways to bring back what belongs to you.

However, if someone has a legitimate excuse and is generally a good-natured person, then you may want to work with him the best that you can. In his heart he may want to pay you back but really can't. There are plenty of examples of really good people who made bad debt decisions.

Principle 34

*Receiving some money from slacking debtors is
better than nothing.*

If a debtor owes money but is having financial problems, then
be open to payment options. A piece here and a piece there may
eventually add up to a complete repayment. Any payment is better
than no payment. However, if the debtor gets too far behind in
payments, then you may want to escalate the situation to a legal
level and/or find a way to cut your losses.

Principle 35

*Sometimes it is more beneficial to make exceptions
to late debtors.*

When someone who is normally of good credit owes you money, be alert to the possibility that there may be excusable external factors in operation. For example, someone's health may be deteriorating (death of a family member, memory loss, stroke, etc.). Let's pretend that you are trying to collect rent from a good long-term tenant but find that the tenant is not returning your calls. After some time, you knock on the door and find him standing in the door. He may appear disheveled, with a little abnormal behavior. However, he is still coherent enough to tell you that he will have the payment for you this week.

A week later, you may receive a call from family members explaining that he has had a series of mini strokes and is now hospitalized. That's when you realize that he wasn't avoiding you but was dealing with the effects of a health problem. He may not have been truly coherent. In this example, you may have to work with the family members until his lease is up to try and help your faithful tenant deal with his new situation.

Principle 36

*Don't lend money to irresponsible and/or
unqualified people and expect to be paid back.*

People who can't handle the pressure of paying debt are more likely to never repay it. Credit agencies, whether for economic or financial entities, are set up for a reason: to assess the ability of people to repay their obligations. Although not a guarantee, a history of someone's credit gives important indications of one's ability to repay. If someone is highly probable of being a credit risk because of her or his credit history, then these potential debtors need to be carefully analyzed for future business. For example, you should not expect continuous on-time payments from a person who already has a history of beating every lender in town out of money.

This principle also applies to lending money to people whose income does not demonstrate the ability to pay back. It is the lenders' responsibility to crunch the numbers and ensure that their potential customers have met all of the required financial criteria of a good loan candidate. Bad loans are mostly the result of loans that should never have been made in the first place.

Principle 37

Paying down debt is another option, along with investing, to maximize wealth.

Reducing debt is an alternative to investing when rates are favorable. With existing debt, there is an option for earning at least as much as your debt interest rate regardless of the economy. Additional principle payments will eliminate the interest that you would have paid. The result in practice is essentially equivalent to earning this interest rate in an investment. Interest saved can be thought of as interest earned.

This principle particularly applies in a severely recessed economy and only if you have the funds to invest. For example, if interest rates are 3 percent for safe investments but your mortgage is charging 7 percent, then you can easily make 4 percent more than the safe investments virtually without risk by paying off the debt (7% - 3% = 4%). As these safe investment rates become closer to zero (or zero), then you can really benefit from retiring your debt by saving even more interest from being paid.

Additional principle on debt should only be repaid when there are no other investments available that can return higher rates than the debt interest rate you are assessed (assuming similar risk levels). In many cases, because credit card interest rates are extremely high (usually 30-plus percent), it is almost always better to pay off these debts first before investing (it is very hard to return more than 10 percent consistently a year let alone 30 percent).

Diversification

Principle 38

Diversification can be applied to everything.

One of the most important lessons learned from modern finance is that an appropriate level of diversification can help you reduce risk while allowing for similar or better returns. One of the best ways to diversify is by combining investments that are negatively correlated, or that have an opposite relationship – for example, buying umbrella and sun-block companies. By diversifying, if you have selected a bad investment, the impact may be reduced if you also have a portfolio of other good investments to help offset its losses. Contrarily, if that was your only investment, then you would be in trouble. This idea applies to any investment, including bonds, collectibles, currency, mutual funds, real estate, and stocks. Diversification also applies to the nonfinancially related aspects of life, such as having many good friends instead of just one. What happens when you need a friend and your only one is unavailable?

Principle 39

Over-diversifying may not increase return or reduce risk.

Diversification can be very useful, but when overdone it can become an impediment to the progress of your wealth. If you purchase every single investment in the known investment universe, you may accomplish many of the goals of diversification. Yet you have to ask yourself if this was really necessary. You may have been able to obtain the same or higher return for the same or lower amount of risk with, let's say, five to one hundred investments (this number is highly debatable). Also, as you increase your number of investments, you must consider that you may be adding overlapping effects (one investment may be the same or similar to another) and thus not reducing your risk at all.

This principle also includes foolishly over-diversifying into investments that you may not be capable of understanding. In his *One Up on Wall Street,* the great investor Peter Lynch has termed this situation *diworseification,* and it is a major reason many big corporations get themselves in trouble. This was particularly evident in the 1960s. Major corporations had used their cash to buy unrelated businesses only to discover later that they didn't know enough about them to be profitable.

Economics

Principle 40

The ideal goal of an economic policy for a nation is to maximize the wealth of its entire people and not that of a specific financial entity.

A nation is only truly wealthy when all of its people are considered in the economic plan. People are motivated more to build a nation's wealth when they can reap a part of its reward. They are generally indifferent when their opportunities of advancement are limited or nonexistent.

A nation that chooses to maximize the wealth of a minority chooses not to maximize the nation's earning capacity. There may now exist a foregone opportunity cost of lost potential innovations that could have been created if the excluded group had been allowed to maximize its wealth.

Principle 41

"A modern nation that chooses not to continuously increase its wealth in both the short and the long term chooses to struggle economically."
(Criniti, *The Necessity of Finance*, 70)

A nation must strive to maximize its short-term and long-term wealth or face the consequences. Nations that choose to minimize wealth take the risk that they will not be able to afford a quality military. A poorly paid inferior military can lead to a higher probability of being conquered by a foreign nation.

Also, a nation that chooses wealth minimization may have indirect negative effects on its people's quality of life. Many famous economists, including Friedrich Hayek and John Maynard Keynes, have also noted that economic policies drastically affect every aspect of human life. If the economic climate of a nation is extremely weak, then that negatively affects the opportunities for financial entities to maximize their wealth. "Economic lessons throughout the ages have taught us that a nation that struggles economically translates to individuals, groups, and organizations of the nation struggling in every aspect of life" (Criniti, *The Necessity of Finance*, 70).

Principle 42

*Every drop of government control is exchanged for
a tablespoon of its people's freedom.*

A government has a special role that plays an important part in any nation. For example, it facilitates tasks that private enterprises have no incentive to do, such as building and maintaining infrastructure. Yet, when the role of government goes beyond what it is mainly responsible for, its people risk losing their freedom, particularly of maximizing their wealth. In a communistic government, the government has total control over its people. This government type eliminates businesses or limits them to only what it allows.

In democratic or republican societies, the government's role is limited (or may start out that way). However, eventually as these societies flourish and become more complicated, the people may allow the government an increasing amount of control over their lives. If this activity is not kept in check, then they risk a conversion to a different form of government and possibly a full-scale totalitarian economy.

Principle 43

Free societies result in improved living conditions starting from the lowest levels of poverty.

In a completely free society (both politically and economically), the poorest people will generally have a better quality of life than in its extreme counterpart. The higher the level of various forms of freedom allowed in a nation, the truer this principle is. When people are allowed to exert their talents in the freest of capacities, then technology is maximized at all levels. The result includes but is not limited to better national infrastructure, better average housing, better food quality, and lower amounts of violence. This principle explains the exponential amount of accomplishments modern America has made over many ancient nations in a short period of time.

The slave nations in history also have demonstrated the power of this principle. Slave nations resulted in good living conditions for the ruling minority and generally low to inhumane conditions for the slaves and the poor. As was pointed out in *The Necessity of Finance*: "Consider the slave nation's lost opportunity of potential wealth if it allowed its entire people the liberty to maximize their wealth. It's not hard to take this one step further and envision ancient nations already at the state of current civilization many years ahead of time" (Criniti, *The Necessity of Finance*, 82).

Principle 44

---

*Product and service specialization is advantageous
for a nation.*

This principle was derived from the concept of the *division of
labor*, which was highly noted by Adam Smith in *The Wealth
of Nations* in 1776. The nation that specializes in producing
a good or service has a better opportunity to become more
efficient in price and time for it than nonspecializing
countries. When a country uses all of its resources to focus on
producing specific products or services, then it will improve
the technology and the techniques required to produce them
cheaper and faster.

This principle works for financial entities as well. A barber is
good at cutting hair and a builder at building because they have
put the time into learning the skills needed for their trade. For this
same reason, nations that utilize many or all of their resources,
including their financial entities, to excel in one field can become
the world's major supplier for that particular product or service.
Some examples include Italian clothing, Japanese cars, and Swiss
watches. As stated in *The Necessity of Finance*: "Thus everyone
committed to persistently searching for better ways to do his or
her job is a scientist in his or her own specialization" (Criniti, *The
Necessity of Finance,* 4).

Principle 45

Economic cycles are naturally required wealth adjustments by economic entities.

It is the natural order of economic entities to encounter bad times and good. The financial entities that are a part of the economic entities sometimes produce more goods or services than is demanded (and vice versa). The result is always a correction of their wealth. The economic entities may have to adjust their economic strategy to align with the current financial situation of its people.

Principle 46

Society's average level of happiness can give you hints of its short-term economic future.

This principle is most applicable to free market societies in a country with equal rights for all of its citizens. When the average people in a given society are much happier than they have been in recent times then this may be a signal for a negative economic adjustment coming soon. This usually is indicated through increasing amounts of leisurely activities (for example traveling), less complaining about money, and higher levels of optimism. This can be titled as the calm before the storm.

Contrarily, when the average people in a given society are much sadder than they have been in recent times, then this may be a signal for a positive economic adjustment. This usually is signaled through increasing amounts of violence, such as homicides, suicides, etc. The trick is to determine when these points of extreme happiness or sadness occur by considering all members of society. For example, the poor generally complain the most about money. However, when you see the rich becoming bankrupt daily and their cries become louder, then that is a significant warning signal that the bottom is almost near.

Principle 47

Everybody's costs are somebody's income.

Current consumption in economic terms translates to spending your money to buy someone else's labor. Every dollar that you spend on buying products and services fuels another person's livelihood, either directly or indirectly. In this manner, at first it may appear easy to conclude that an economy can maximize its wealth by encouraging its people to continuously spend. This argument, however, does not consider other important factors, particularly the effects of debt.

Principle 48

Successful businesses produce wealth for a nation.

The more successful a business is in producing desirable goods and services (as opposed to goods or services that nobody wants) for a nation, the more wealth it creates and circulates within that nation. Its success creates a chain of employment because it may spend more money on expanding its operations. More profits may lead to more wealth for a nation (for example, by increasing employment and having more income to tax, etc.). The more productive successful businesses a nation produces, the wealthier it may become.

Principle 49

A wealthy population creates an overall healthy population.

In a free capitalistic society, there will always be people with more money than others as this is the natural order of things. There are all different degrees of laborers, from lazy ones to workaholics. Assuming a nation's people started out equal in wealth, the hardest-working people will generally always make more money than the laziest. Based on labor only, these people will probably be the wealthiest.

You need wealthy people in a free economic society. A common fallacy that exists is that the rich are useless to the poor as they provide nothing and take everything. To understand this fallacy, one must imagine if you had no wealthy people in a country and the consequences this tragedy would bring. The quality of life would disintegrate as the wealthiest people move all of their money (and their ability to employ with that money) somewhere else.

Wealthy people have the power to employ and invest. The rich who employ and invest well will generally remain wealthy, and vice versa for those who don't. When you remove the rich from a country, then you have essentially cut the legs off a nation and forced it to walk on its hands.

Principle 50

The ones who amass and maintain wealth are generally the best fit in the struggle to employ it.

Wealthy financial managers are a valuable asset to a nation if they know how to employ and invest their wealth to have a positive impact on the greatest number of people and our planet. Amassing wealth is a tough accomplishment for any financial entity, but it takes a special breed of people to maintain and employ it well. The challenge of economics is for a nation or its divisions to find better ways to ensure that the most ethically sound financial leaders rise and stay at the top (or at least until they are replaced with even better financial leaders). This special group of people is one of the nation's most precious assets as their skillset keeps the jobs of a nation circulating.

Principle 51

*The more economic failures a nation learns from,
the stronger that nation becomes.*

Economic education, like that of other sciences, is perpetual. There is always a new situation that may appear to jeopardize existing theories. Nations throughout history have made many economic mistakes. The results of these have led to the stronger economic policies that exist in many of our modern most powerful nations. Although far from economic perfection (hopefully, this book will provide nations with more enlightenment), we must admit that our great nations have learned something and have improved somewhat from their mistakes.

The biggest example of this is that forms of totalitarianism, such as communism, definitely don't work in the long run. The collapse of the Soviet Union was a lesson that will be permanently stamped in economic history. Any country that makes that attempt again deserves the consequences it should have avoided. In the long run, if the new Russia reexamines and improves on the flaws of the old economic system, it should become a very powerful nation again.

Principle 52

Inevitably, globalization will unite the economic goals of all nations.

As technology is making the world smaller, it is an unavoidable conclusion that the goals of all nations will eventually have to become unified into one if we are to survive peacefully on this planet. That is, the goal of economics, which is "to continuously maximize wealth for a nation or a division of a nation," (Criniti, *The Necessity of Finance*, 68) may eventually be restated: "to continuously maximize wealth for the planet." At that point, economics may even be renamed to something like "Earthonomics."

Maximization of wealth has brought our civilization to its current form. Why would it stop here? As stated in *The Necessity of Finance*: "The possibility of enhancing personal wealth has generally always been the carrot on the end of the stick enticing people to use their creativity to advance humanity. The possibility of enhancing personal wealth will also be the fuel to help the human race reach its maximum potential in the future" (Criniti, *The Necessity of Finance*, 4).

Ethics

Principle 53

The price of great wealth is responsibility.

People of average wealth may only look at wealth accumulation as a means to an end for fulfilling their own personal goals. But really financially intelligent, wealthy people know that there is a higher justification for wealth beyond financial independence. Pretend that you had a billion dollars. After you set aside money needed to meet all of your life's essentials, what do you do with the rest?

Once you become really wealthy, be prepared to give and lead. J. Paul Getty, once the world's richest man, said it best: "His aim should be to create and operate businesses which contribute their share to the progressive upward movement of the world's economy, and which thus work to make life better for all. Therein lies the justification for wealth, and therefrom does the working businessman derive the greatest sense of satisfaction" (Getty, *How To Be Rich*, 196). Also, as described about John Templeton in *The Templeton Plan*, "His attitude toward his worldly success involved a sense of stewardship, a belief that what you have is not actually yours but is held in trust for the good of all humanity" (Templeton, *The Templeton Plan*, 165).

Principle 54

A good reputation pays a high rate of return.

It may take you many decades to earn the respect of your peers. This may be derived from years of demonstrating your loyalty, doing the right things, helping others, and honoring your word. These actions form the characteristics of highly regarded people. Society shows its respect for people with a good reputation by asking for their advice in life's most challenging moments.

For example, in times of dire need, a client will disclose her or his deepest secrets to the most well-respected attorney, financial planner, or surgeon. These individuals have built a reputation so solid that people will freely give them their trust in exchange for help. This is a privilege generally only given to either a rare, highly reputable breed or the slickest frauds. In the long term, it is only the continuously well-respected individual or business that will benefit from earning society's trust and wealth.

Principle 55

Unethical behavior may sometimes create large short-term wealth but always destroys most or all of long-term wealth.

Older successful companies are still in business for a good reason. Businesses that build their foundation on deception are generally not open very long. Their customers and investors can't be fooled forever. Eventually, when they find out they are dealing with a crook; they will take their business elsewhere. If financial entities unethically manipulate society to maximize their own wealth, eventually when the truth prevails, as it always does, most or all of their wealth will deteriorate to nothing.

There are plenty of examples of this, particularly in corporate America. For example, think of how much wealth a company like Enron would have had by now if it was still in business. How much wealth would they have if they were in business another fifty years? How about another one hundred years? All of this long-term wealth was sacrificed for a quick short-term gain. **It is much more profitable to do the right thing, besides the fact that it is the right thing to do.**

Principle 56

Some people will do anything to deprive you of your wealth.

There are some people out there that are capable of performing unimaginable unethical acts. For the average person with some sort of moral compass, it is difficult to comprehend the possibility of another person doing these things. But don't let your guard down because that is how you become their victim. These despicable people usually operate in scam markets of all levels, ranging from counterfeit checks to Ponzi schemes.

To give you an example of this principle, I will tell you briefly of something that happened to me once. This example does not by any means represent the absolute bottom of the bad barrel as there are many frauds that are capable of much worse. One cold winter in Philadelphia, I was approached by an elderly man in a supermarket parking lot. He asked me for money that he claimed was going to a homeless shelter for older people like him. As there was a major snow storm the day before, there were many people who had to relocate because they didn't have power. This man's story was told with absolute perfection even after deep inquiry. He knew everything about this particular shelter he was representing, including its address, its phone numbers, and the names of the people who worked there. He even had a false ID and literature from this shelter. Of course after I gave him some money, I found out from the shelter that he had no affiliation with them.

How can one stoop so low? How many good innocent people did he scam? Sadly, this world has people in it that would steal from their own parents. You must always be on guard for these lowly people. They will clean out your wealth before you know what hit you.

Principle 57

Every laborer can make this world a better place to live and love.

Almost every occupation, as mundane as it may appear, is interconnected with others in some way. Laborers from these occupations complement each other by exchanging their time from a unique task. The end result is our modern civilization, where we can use the money from our own specialization to shop from the infinite fruits of the labor of others. The point of this principle is to acknowledge the contributions of hard work made by others in jobs different from your own.

If you see someone doing a job that you may never want to do, such as cleaning a dirty street at five o'clock in the morning on a cold wintery night, it is important to appreciate that man's work. If it wasn't for him, then walking down that street would be a much more unpleasant experience. As John Templeton put it: "Every individual is like a thread in a beautiful tapestry with a vital contribution to make, not only to the sustenance of life as we know it, but in the creation and development of more beneficial expressions of life" (Templeton, *Worldwide Laws of Life*, 136).

Principle 58

The risks of the agency problem are applicable to all economic and financial entities.

The agency problem exists when agents of an economic or a financial entity place their personal goals before the entity they represent. An example would be a corporate executive who made a company decision that resulted in him making more profits than his employers. Due to inevitable flaws of the human character, the agency problem cannot be eliminated, so it must be controlled.

As expressed in *The Necessity of Finance*: "This issue is so important because it is always present in any situation where someone is given responsibility of managing wealth for someone else, and even the nicest people on earth have a chance of not doing the right thing in certain situations, particularly in financial situations" (Criniti, *The Necessity of Finance*, 173). Also, "it is an innate instinct for a financial manager to have the constant urge to place his or her survival needs before others'. Rare, exceptional financial managers are able to control this urge and successfully complete their assigned tasks while fulfilling their moral responsibilities to the client" (Criniti, *The Necessity of Finance*, 174).

Financial Psychology

Principle 59

The gain or loss of money enhances one's emotional state.

The gain or loss of money (and other forms of wealth) has the ability to accelerate or decelerate the speed of one's emotions. The more money that was gained, the faster one may become happier. For example, if a person just found out that she won the lottery then her cheeks may glow with joy within seconds. If she was already happy before she found out then she will become even happier. Contrarily, a sad man will become a little sadder upon loss of some money but very sad upon loss of a lot of money. Casino environments usually showcase this principle in its extremes. You can sit at a casino table and watch an already glum sad man become miserable instantly upon the loss of his last dollar.

Principle 60

A loss of money has stronger psychological consequences than a gain of the same amount of money.

Gaining money can excite someone in various degrees depending on the value of the gain. However, losing the same amount of money will generally have a stronger impact in the exact opposite emotional direction. This principle was mentioned many years ago by John Burr Williams: "If it is true that gambling is irrational, and that the loss of a dollar hurts more than the gain of a dollar helps, then a fee for risk-bearing should reasonably be expected wherever risks are borne in the economic world" (Williams, *The Theory of Investment Value*, 486).

A good way to illustrate this principle is to take another visit to the casino, the financialist's laboratory. Imagine a man who has only $150 to spend and has just entered the casino floor. This man knows that with this amount of money he can buy the following: one night in a comfortable hotel room, a dinner buffet, a short night out with a few drinks, a nice breakfast the next day at the local diner, and money for gas and tolls to drive roundtrip from his home. All in all, this amount of money can give him a much needed small vacation to relax for two days and one night.

If this man decides to bet all of his money on black or red on the roulette table, then two major outcomes can happen: he will double his money or lose it all. Sure, an extra $150 would be nice for him as he can stay and relax at the casino for an extra night. However, if he loses all of his money, then this man risks facing a relatively more uncomfortable situation: going home early and not getting to enjoy his much needed one night of relaxation.

Principle 61

*The pursuit of making money can become an
addiction that generally increases with wealth.*

Money is equivalent to the strongest drug never yet invented. A really poor man generally thinks about money for reasons of necessity. A really rich man generally thinks about money as a game. The more the rich earn, the more they may want to earn as they may desire a higher score. As their wealth increases, the game gets more interesting. This behavior will continue until the wealthy man reaches the highest level of his desired wealth, ranging from financially independent to the richest person in the world. Generally, only then does the rich man's pursuit start to shift to other interests, particularly charity. However, his addiction to money may reignite if his charitable donations have caused his wealth to decline to an intolerable level.

Also, note that poor people may be addicted to making money as well. However, they generally may become more addicted as they make more money. So if they start poor with an addiction to money, then this may become magnified when they are wealthy.

Principle 62

The long-term consequences of therapy shopping far outweigh any temporary gain of quick psychological relief.

Spendthrifts sometimes shop when they are feeling sad as shopping may make them happier (or has made them happier at one point in time). This type of behavior becomes addictive and causes one to desire to shop every time that there is pain in life. However, shopping to relieve psychological pain may only be a temporary cure for the symptom but never a complete cure for the real problem. In the long run, the spendthrifts create mounds of debt and/or deplete their assets to feed their shopaholic addiction. Thus, the temporary solution eventually becomes the bigger problem.

Principle 63

Accepting gifts may create unforeseen psychological consequences.

Understand the potential psychological consequences when you accept gifts (particularly larger gifts) from someone, especially family. That is, the donor of a gift (the person who gives a gift) may feel a sense of entitlement to you and your wealth. The money the donor laid down, even if it was many years ago, may make the person feel as if he or she has special rights and privileges over you forever or until that money is given back. You may always be indebted to the so-called "kindness" of the donor.

Rare donors know that a true gift should have no strings attached and live by that principle. However, that is generally not the case. Many donors will often pull the wild card of "remember what I did for you" whenever they feel the need to. This may be an emotional strain for the person who accepted the gift (the donee). Unconsciously, by accepting gifts from certain people, you have essentially returned the favor by giving them an opportunity to control your life. An example may include adults who accept a "gift" of a mortgage-free residential property from their wealthy parents. In exchange, they may allow their parents to control every major decision for their house and their children.

Principle 64

Major economic events generally cause everlasting impressions on the future financial affairs of its survivors.

That is, financial entities that have survived through extreme economic events, such as depressions, may manage all future financial behavior in relation to these experiences. For example, those that have survived the Great Depression, on average, tend to be more frugal as they may know firsthand of the difficulties of not having any money. Even if these individuals become very wealthy, they generally may still exhibit the frugal characteristics that have resonated in them since their experience with surviving a greatly depressed economy. Psychologically, they may have permanently prepared themselves to avoid poverty to the best of their ability.

Principle 65

One's moral beliefs outrank their money in priority.

It is our human, internalized processes that allow money to be so powerful. Thus, it should be no surprise that these same processes have the power to weaken our feelings toward money. Assuming one has a moral compass, a person has the power to override any financial decisions when they conflict with her or his beliefs in what is right or wrong. As an extreme example, a person who doesn't believe in harming others probably would not accept a job to kill for money.

Alternatively, a woman may choose not to buy urgent prescription medicine at her local pharmacy because she was mistreated there by an employee many years ago. She believes that a good customer should be treated with respect. She now may have to drive a farther distance for her prescription drugs. Spitefully, she would rather take an additional health risk and pay a higher cost than to give her local pharmacy any business. To her, it's not about the money; it's about the moral principle.

Principle 66

*The public mind is generally content with feeling
the universal emotion of each economic period,
regardless of whether it is bad or good.*

This principle falls under the umbrella science of group psychology and pertains to what is called "herd behavior." The majority of humans tend to make decisions that conform to those made by their few leaders. As the economy flows through its cycles of bad and good times, the general sentiment of financial entities tends to compliment it. If the economy is performing very well, then the general feelings of the masses are happiness and optimism.

Contrarily, the opposite occurs in negative economies. The negative times are best described by Humphrey Neill, a leader in contrarian thinking: "People then wish to enjoy their misery. They do not wish that wet blanket removed" (Neill, *The Art of Contrary Thinking*, 118). I suspect the reason this principle may be true is that people generally try to resist too much change too fast, especially when dealing with their emotions. When times are tough too long, it may be hard for people to adjust again to brighter days. The financial entities of a nation go through an "economic mourning" of the loss of their national wealth, even if it didn't affect them directly. Like any mourning, it is a process that takes time to heal.

General Economics and Finance Miscellaneous

Principle 67

When economic or financial problems are bad, it is possible that they can always get worse.

Even the best economic or financial plan is subjected to external forces that are out of your control. It is best to always be prepared for the worst-case scenario. Every time you make an investment or take out a loan, you should ask yourself, "If this plan doesn't succeed, what will I do?" "Could I survive?" There are so many situations that can change your fortune in a moment's notice that you could never have foreseen coming, such as a major lawsuit or a new unfavorable tax law.

Principle 68

There is no such thing as a permanent Caesar.

Even if you reach the top, you may not stay there. It is hard enough to become wealthy (assuming humble beginnings); it is, at minimum, equally hard to maintain your wealth. The faces of the top wealthiest list change frequently for various reasons. This is why it is extremely important to learn not only how to make wealth but how to keep it. There are things that wealthy people shouldn't do if they want to stay wealthy, for example, becoming a spendthrift. Yes, billionaires can go broke too.

Principle 69

Always having income is a guard against wealth minimization.

No matter what, always have some form of money coming in. Life is expensive as it costs money to live in our society (food, rent, etc.). With an income, at least you will have something to pay the bills (and something is better than nothing).

I dedicate this principle to people who would rather be unemployed until their dream job falls onto them. In the meantime (months or maybe decades), they have dug themselves into extreme debt to finance their lifestyle. To avoid this problem, temporarily you may have to take on difficult underpaid work that nobody else wants to do. But at least if you have some income, then you could avoid any unnecessary liabilities from accumulating. In this situation, you could also have some spending money while simultaneously searching for your real career job.

Principle 70

*Economic and financial managers should learn
from all wealth-management mistakes.*

Some economic and financial mistakes cost nothing to learn and some may cost a lot. However, if you learn from each mistake, you will increase your probability of increasing and/or maintaining your wealth. If you don't learn from your mistake, then you may lose money and an opportunity for advancing your economic or financial education. What doesn't kill you can make you stronger if you learn from your failure.

Principle 71

Mastering the science of finance can help you to control your own wealth.

Only you can manage your own wealth with absolute certainty that it is allocated the way you intended it. Who should care more about your money than you? Finance teaches you how to manage your wealth to maximize it. Personal money management allows for maximum control and direction of your financial freedom.

Principle 72

Economic and financial advice is only as good as the advisor.

Everyone should learn how to manage her or his money. However, for those who don't want to do this and would rather have someone else assist them, at least ensure that this person (or people) is highly credible and has a solid track record. You want to know everything about your potential economic or financial manager. Specifically, you should want to know if this person has demonstrated wealth management successfully through personal example. What does this person's portfolio look like? If economic or financial managers can't manage their own money successfully, how can you expect them to do any better for you?

Principle 73

*Knowing your bottom-line price ahead gives you
an edge in any negotiation process.*

Don't ever make an offer to buy or sell anything without spending time to determine your buy or sell price first. With this price, you can reflect better on potential negotiation outcomes depending on your strategy. For a floating negotiation strategy, generally lower or raise your offer or counteroffer price proportionately to your bottom-line price relative to your opponent's proposal. For example, your bottom-line price might be to sell an asset for $1,000. Let's pretend the offer to buy comes in at $800. To get to your bottom-line price, assuming that you both meet in the middle, you will need to add 20 percent more to your bottom-line price to match the buyer's 20 percent less ($1,000 - $800 = $200/$1,000 = 20%). Thus, if you counteroffer at $1,200 ($1,000 x 1.2), then you may compromise in the middle at your $1,000 goal. For a fixed negotiation strategy, your bottom-line price is your firm price regardless of your opponent's offer or counteroffer.

Principle 74

How much money you make is not as important as how much money you keep.

As strange as it is to believe, money makers throughout time have spent much of their focus solely on the amount of money they make from their line of work. However, the bottom-line number is the amount that tells the truer picture of the fruits of one's labor. Your actual gross income is subjected to many forces before it is brought down to reality. That is, you may have many work-related expenses that were required in order to make any income, such as buying tools or travel expenses. This money spent is a cost that washes away any gains. What about other important items like insurance, interest on needed business loans, and/or taxes?

There are many financial entities with extraordinary gross incomes that become reduced to practically nothing when all appropriate deductions are made. This principle is important because you need to recognize that what you may appear to make is only an illusion when all factors are considered. Thus, with a realistic income picture, you can avoid overspending on things that you can't afford (but think that you can).

Principle 75

Wealth and intelligence are not always correlated.

Don't assume that because a person is wealthy he or she is also generally intelligent. A poor man can be brilliant and a rich man can be a moron. Wealth presents plenty of opportunities for improving various levels of intelligence if desired. Nevertheless, some wealthy people may not capitalize on these opportunities as they may become content with an easy lifestyle.

It is not hard to understand why wealth may create the illusion that someone is generally intelligent. The person may have been able to afford to go to an academically prestigious school. By association, it is logical to think that a person who attended a smart school must also be smart.

Contrarily, history has provided plenty of examples of extremely bright people who were born and raised in poverty. Poverty can teach someone life's greatest lessons, for example, how to deal with the daily monetary struggles that may be unknown to the very wealthy. However, regardless of current wealth status, at a certain point, wealth generally follows naturally for the person who strives to have the highest level of intelligence in her or his specialty.

Principle 76

Gossip has value.

Pay attention to what people all around you are saying (even people that you don't know). In every conversation, there are subtle hints of how to better manage your money and time. This applies to all levels, ranging from a business idea to forecasting economic cycles. People's everyday conversations give indications of economic moods and individual thoughts on wealth. Also, trained economists or financialists can analyze the general and personal sentiment on wealth to improve their understanding of their sciences.

Principle 77

As long as politicians exist, they will have a role in the allocation of a nation's wealth.

Government tax revenues historically have been spent on the interests of a small wealthy minority. As much as one would like to believe that the money is spent on the common wealth of all the people, generally this is not the case. Particularly in many modern nations, citizens' tax money is directed toward accomplishing the goals of those who spend the most lobbying for certain actions. Politicians are usually the matchmakers between laws that were heavily lobbied for and what the general public really wants. These compromises, along with the agency problem, are major reasons why government inefficiencies exist for common sense situations.

Principle 78

Wealth is attracted to cities.

In general, you will find your greatest opportunities to build wealth in cities versus suburbia or the country. The center of any city usually has more people living and working there than any other part of that metropolitan area. Modern civilization has created the city as a method to facilitate the everyday operations of the majority of businesses of a given area. This is where markets make exchanges, including the employment market.

However, if you are trying to decide what city to live in, you should consider that the largest city does not always have the best odds of maximizing wealth as there may be too much competition and an unfavorable cost of living. Excessive population can also erode your quality of life. A balanced environment may be ideal, but this also depends on how much urban life you can tolerate.

Principle 79

*When all options are bad, then it may be a good
time to take a chance to improve your wealth.*

A person with nothing to lose has a great probability of making
a gain. Even if that person makes the slightest progress, it is
progress over zero. There are many ways to apply this principle
in infinite situations. For example, consider a woman who just
lost her long-term, dead-end job and there are no similar jobs on
the market. Maybe technology has eliminated the demand for this
kind of work. She may now have the opportunity to start her own
dream business. This bad situation may be a fortune in disguise.
Her schedule has been freed with the time needed to focus on
something that may make her happy.

Principle 80

"An ounce of prevention is worth a pound of cure."
– Benjamin Franklin

No book of this nature would be complete without some wisdom from Ben Franklin. This principle may overlap with some planning principles, yet it is also a great lesson on its own. It is important to manage your wealth to reduce or eliminate your unnecessary risk. Risk is better managed by being proactive now rather than being reactive to a bigger problem later. For example, consider the effects of having homeowner's insurance if your home was to catch fire. If you have insurance, the biggest problem is paying the premiums every month. But now that you need it, it has prevented a financial catastrophe. The cost of the small premiums was nothing compared to what it would have cost you to rebuild your house.

Principle 81

Wealth is always shifting.

Every day fortunes are lost and made. The wealth of all economic and financial entities changes daily in varying degrees and forms. This is best explained if we can pretend that everybody in the world starts out with equal amounts of money. They will not end in the same position upon their death. One major reason is that there is a finite amount of money at any given moment and products and services must be continuously bought and sold, sometimes at higher or lower prices, in order to survive in our modern civilization. For every unit of money that you gain, someone else must have lost that unit. They may get it back from someone else later (for example, in another transaction), but for now that specific money is gone.

As an example, if you buy some groceries that cost $100, then that money flows from you to the seller. Technically, although your cash has decreased, your wealth is still the same because you now have $100 in groceries. But as you will either eat the food or it will perish, this event will eventually result in your wealth being reduced by $100. Alternatively, if you invest $100 in a stock then this money, called capital, flows out of your pocket into the sellers. In this case, this stock may eventually sell for a higher amount later, returning your capital plus a return on your investment.

Principle 82

*Putting all economic and financial affairs in
writing helps to guard against unexpected issues.*

This particularly applies to all investments and liabilities, especially with family and partners. Contracts dictate when a problem arises. By spending time in the beginning of any major economic or financial decision to lay out the important details, you may avoid any ambiguous interpretations later and ensure a more successful implementation of your original decision.

Principle 83

The terms in contracts can be more powerful than the stated interest rates.

Earning a higher rate of return on your investment or paying a lower interest rate payment on your debt should not be your only focus. What a rate may give you, a term can exponentially take away. For example, you can have a loan with a low interest rate that is taken away when certain conditions kick in (i.e., after an introductory period of time such as twelve months). Alternatively, you may invest in a restricted bond that pays a high interest rate. However, maybe you can't sell it for ten years without a substantial penalty.

Principle 84

Regularly taking account of your wealth allows you to quickly remedy any immediate issues.

Frequent monitoring of your wealth can help you to eliminate any major discrepancies that may arise. If there are any issues, they can be dealt with more efficiently the sooner they are detected. There are infinite examples where someone's bank account or credit card has accrued sudden unauthorized transactions. These are usually the result of fraud or transactional errors. If you don't check your accounts, these activities will slip by unnoticed and result in unnecessary loss of wealth.

Principle 85

It is important to always inspect your bill before you pay.

Accidents happen and items on a bill are sometimes reported incorrectly. You may overpay after the fact and the likelihood of receiving the difference back may decrease over time. For example, you may have been charged twice at the supermarket for an item and not realized it if you didn't look at the receipt. It is much easier to show proof of the error while you are still there.

Another good example is when the items on a bill don't add up to the total correctly. It is bad to assume the total is always correct, because the computers or the people who made the bill may have made a mistake.

Principle 86

Premature spending should be rewarded with a discount and only implemented when the other party is highly trusted.

When given a choice, do not pay for goods or services before you receive them, unless a discount is applied. The time value of money needs to be considered in every transaction. The discount will compensate you for the interest that you could have earned on the money before the actual transaction was made. For example, if you were to purchase your summer vacation six months in advance, then you should be given a discount (maybe x percent) for committing your money when it could have been earning a return elsewhere.

Also, you should trust the company or person that you are dealing with. When you give people money for goods or services that you will be receiving too far in the future, this always leaves temptation for the other party to not complete the transaction. If they are reputable, then you don't need to worry as much. However, if they are untrustworthy and they receive the money before the job is done (or goods received) then you may never hear from them again (and not receive your paid-for goods or services).

Principle 87

Measure financial success not only by total wealth achieved but by the number of obstacles one has overcome.

The title of "successful" cannot be inherited; it must be earned. A woman born out of poverty who became a billionaire from her specialized talent may be properly labeled a success. But if her rich children add absolutely no value to this world and live off her wealth, they cannot claim to be successful also. People who desire to be successful, poor or rich, need to earn their respect by demonstrating how they manage their talents and wealth when individually faced with adversity. Success is a personal quality that must be measured independently with every new generation.

Principle 88

Not everyone is meant to be wealthy.

We are all built with different strengths and weaknesses. Becoming very wealthy requires many characteristics that many people do not have or do not care to have, for example, the ability to plan, to understand finance, and to work hard. Even those who appear to have these characteristics may have other forces working against them, for example, psychological forces. **The gambler types may know well every lesson in this book. Yet all this knowledge may not prevent them from betting their next paycheck on their favorite horse.**

Principle 89

---

*It is important to beware of individuals with
extraordinary influencing abilities.*

There are rare exceptional salespeople with a special skill to convince people to do things they may not have ordinarily done under normal circumstances. They may convince even the savviest to sign their fortunes away. If you encounter a person like this and you get lured by their pitch, consider taking some time to think about whatever decision you need to make (a good rule is at least twenty-four hours). People usually come to their senses after some time alone and a good night's rest. In Edwin Lefevre's *Reminiscences of a Stock Operator*, his character, who was based on the great stock operator Jesse Livermore, stated, "You can never bank on there being but one remarkable salesman in the world or on complete immunization from the influence of personality" (Lefevre, *Reminiscences of a Stock Operator*, 133).

Principle 90

Patience is rewarded to those who wait to buy new, highly demanded products or services.

Waiting for the price of a new product or service (especially technologically related) to come down after its first entrance to markets may save you plenty of money. The markups are usually extraordinary when supply is low but the demand is very high. New competition will eventually be created that balances the unequal forces and hence lowers the price for the customers. As the great economist Adam Smith put it: "The increase of demand, besides, though in the beginning it may sometimes raise the price of goods, never fails to lower it in the long run" (Smith, *The Wealth of Nations*, 950).

There are circumstances where it may be more practical to pay higher prices then to wait for when prices are reduced. For example, assume you wanted to eat authentic Chinese food and there was only one Chinese restaurant in your area. If you wait for competition to lower the overall Chinese food prices, then you may deprive yourself of the instant gratification desired now.

Principle 91

In fair transactions, prices are also a reflection of the quality of the goods or services bought.

The price of a product or service includes many factors, particularly demand. But quality is also an important consideration. If you buy something at a cheap price, e.g., a house made out of wood, then you may be getting an inferior product or service relative to its more expensive counterparts, i.e., the same house made out of brick or stone. Market prices generally reflect the amount of labor and skill needed. The more labor and skill that it takes, then the higher the price will be. When this principle is not true in the short run, then in time the prices of a product or service will usually be corrected to reflect what it's really worth. For example, if a price is too high relative to what the seller is offering, then the seller will receive fewer sales until the price is lowered.

Principle 92

When you discuss your business in public, you invite the public into your business.

Be very mindful of what you say when you are in the presence of people capable of hearing your financial affairs who shouldn't be. You can never be too certain as to what they can do with your information. You may have just voluntarily disclosed something important to your biggest competitor. It is much safer to discuss your wealth in private and eliminate the risk.

Also, there are many people who speak about their wealth in public with an attitude of indifference. A common defense to ignoring this principle is, "Who cares? What can they do with my information anyway?" Even if you are very poor and think that things can't get worse, if your identity is stolen because of a loose tongue, you may have summoned in your worst nightmare.

Principle 93

Large-scale opportunities to deceive the masses out of their wealth are developed at least once every generation.

At least once every generation a unique mania (or a bubble) is formed that attracts a massive obsession to maximize wealth. Unfortunately, the newer generation is fresh bait for certain savvy economic and financial managers. The result from these manias is that the majority of people lose a large part of their wealth for not being able to recognize the warning signs of market overvaluation and/or a large scam. Usually, the people that always get hurt the most include the overly optimistic youth who have never encountered this situation before and older people who have but never learned. Until the principles in economics and finance are learned by the masses at a young age, new opportunities to deceive the financially inexperienced and uneducated may always exist.

Principle 94

The more risk you take, the more you can lose or make.

This is certainly one of the most well-known lessons in economics and finance. There is a reward-and-risk relationship that exists, particularly in investment situations. That is, if you select investments that are considered risky, like a stock, then you may make a lot of money or you may lose everything. Contrarily, if you select investments that are considered safe, for example, Treasury bonds, then you may not earn much, but at least your principle is not reduced. You are trading off less return for less risk.

However, when you consider inflation, this situation can be viewed another way. It can be argued that investing in theoretically safer investments is really risky because your money is highly subjected to losing purchasing power from higher prices. This argument considers investments that can keep up with or beat inflation as a safer proposition.

Principle 95

Ignoring the lessons in economics and finance equates to welcoming a lifetime of struggles for a nation and its people.

Economics and finance deal with wealth management but from two different perspectives; thus, they need to be separated into their own sciences. Nevertheless, understanding these two sciences is crucial to the preservation of every living thing in this world. In our modern civilization, to struggle economically and financially means to struggle in every aspect of life.

Economics is not finance and finance is not economics, but they are both extremely important. "If you strip away the prospects of learning better ways to manage the wealth of a nation, as in economics, or the wealth of an individual, a group, or an organization, as in finance, our present wealth-dependent civilization might fully regress" (Criniti, *The Necessity of Finance*, 6).

Principle 96

"Ignoring the lessons of finance equates to welcoming a lifetime of financial struggles for an individual, a group, or an organization." (Criniti, *The Necessity of Finance,* 48)

Those who learn and implement the principles in finance have the highest odds of maximizing wealth and avoiding the difficult life associated with poverty. Finance must be continuously studied and practiced to increase your chance of survival in modern civilization. As well stated in George Clason's *The Richest Man in Babylon*: "Gold is reserved for those who know its laws and abide by them" (Clason, *The Richest Man in Babylon*, 80). John Burr Williams also was familiar with this principle: "Just as army strategists study military history with great care, and refight in imagination the campaigns of famous generals, so should the thoughtful investor study financial history with great care and remake in imagination the transactions of former markets" (Williams, *The Theory of Investment Value*, 511).

Principle 97

Learning well the economic and financial tools of your time better prepares you to build your road to wealth independence.

As civilization evolves, the wealth-management tools that we use change. Thousands of years ago, money was in its infancy and was represented by simple items like jewelry and sea shells. Now we have a more extensive variety of monetary forms, ranging from checks to various coins. There is also a historical record amount of investments to select from. It is important to keep up to speed with these changes so that you know what all your options are and how to utilize them if necessary. This gives you an edge on maximizing your wealth by expanding your range of opportunities.

Principle 98

"Financial products should be designed to help make society function better, not worse."
(Criniti, *The Necessity of Finance,* 202)

The past one hundred years has witnessed the growth of so many new financial products and services that they can be overwhelming. There are some of them that may have contributed little or nothing to society except maybe to make it more complicated. These products should be reviewed to determine if there can be a better way to reinvent them to make them more useful. If not, it is better to eliminate them to avoid having economic and financial systems too confusing to manage.

Health

Principle 99

---

*It is hard to enjoy great wealth when you are
deprived of great health.*

Lessons from elderly retirees, especially many centenarians, indicate that wealth means very little when your health won't allow you to enjoy it. What good is having a lot of money if your health prevents you from spending it the way that you want to? This lesson should resonate especially with people who will continuously overwork themselves to earn more wealth without any consideration for their health. Eventually, their behavior may have caused irreversible damage to their health, which may impede them from performing ideal retirement activities, like boating or traveling. In the end, all of their life's work may not have resulted in their desired reward of a beautiful retirement.

Principle 100

"In general, higher levels of wealth provide an individual with a better path to higher levels of health." (Criniti, *The Necessity of Finance,* 184)

Even in historical times when the medical community had little understanding of its specialty, wealthy people still had other better resources than the poor to maintain a higher level of health, for example better food sources or a stronger house. With modern medicine capable of doing extraordinary things, wealthier people who can afford better medical care may live longer than a person in similar health that can't. It doesn't mean that a wealthy person will choose this option; it just means that it exists. A wealthy person also can choose to smoke, overeat, do drugs, and never exercise. Current medicine can do little for the people who do little to help themselves. However, in general, money can buy better doctors and medicine, especially for vitally important surgeries (like open-heart surgery).

Human Resources

Principle 101

Employers who disrespect employees should expect its reciprocation.

Employees are assets, but they are also humans. They live and thrive on appreciation of their work, however insignificant it may appear. J. Paul Getty's advice on how to reward their work is as follows: "Praise should always be given in public, criticism should always be delivered in private" (Getty, *How To Be Rich*, 51). It is important to treat employees with respect as it will create many powerful long-term benefits for the business. If employees feel appreciated for their work and are treated well by a company, then they will more than likely return the favor through higher productivity and spreading higher morale among coworkers. Contrarily, mistreating employees, especially in front of their peers, can create permanent resentment.

It is also equally important that an employee show the same amount of respect for the employer. Inequality of respect between employees and employers, like friendships, may eventually lead to a bad break in the relationship.

Principle 102

It is important to continuously test all employees for integrity.

Dishonest and disloyal employees will bankrupt a business quickly. It is very important to ensure that all employees have the highest quality of character and are working diligently to meet the company's goals. As people's opinion of their employer may change, it is crucial for a business to recognize the warning signs of a problem employee. A typically honest person can become a thief under certain circumstances. Random tests should be used occasionally (for example, spotters) to measure personnel's alignment with the company's goals.

Principle 103

A business is only as strong as its weakest employee.

Any business of any size can become bankrupt quickly through the incompetent action of any employee. Generally, the more power the employee has, the more damage that he or she can do to a business. For example, if the chief financial officer or any other executive implements a bad financial decision, then that could quickly become catastrophic. However, even the lowest-ranked employees can do or say something to the customer and create an irreparable bad reputation for a company and permanent loss of business. There is an infinite number of scenarios where any representative of a business can ruin a company directly or indirectly. This is why competency and integrity screening is crucial for every potential employee.

Principle 104

Employers should only hire employees if their labor will be profitable.

This principle may help the job seekers become more realistic with assessing their desired income from an employer. Intelligent employers know that they eventually must make more money on their employee's labor than the cost of her or his salary. If you cannot add value to a company, then a company has no intellectual reason for hiring you as it would lose money to do so. Businesses are created to make a profit and not a loss. The more an employee can add wealth to its owners, the more he or she can command in wages.

International Finance

Principle 105

Financial entities should know well the nations where they store their wealth.

You should intensely study the country where you plan on conducting your financial affairs, particularly while investing or operating a business. There are many unique financial risks to consider when managing wealth in foreign countries, including currency and political risk. It is very important to research a country's culture, economic situation, laws, etc., before implementing any major decisions. For example, it might be considered very disrespectful to the people of a nation to open a business that sells something that is taboo or offending to their culture. This business will probably not become successful and might even cause physical retaliation by its people.

Investing

Principle 106

Never invest in anything that you do not understand.

This principle has been recognized by many of the greatest investors, including Peter Lynch and Donald Trump. It is extremely important for you to know your investment. You should be able to explain and defend it in a minute or less at a fifth-grade level.

For example, there are many professional real estate investors who will experimentally invest and lose money in the stock market. They will do this without any prior knowledge of these investments. Instead, they should have focused on the investments that they knew better. If they wanted to venture out into different investments, then they should have done their research first.

Principle 107

Always judge a book by its cover and its contents.

Unfortunately, too many people ignore the wise saying "don't judge a book by its cover." If an investment sounds too good to be true, then it usually is good enough to convince the naïve or fantasy chasers. But investing should not be done in ignorance or without being grounded to reality.

It doesn't matter how good an investment may appear at first glance. Although perception is important, investment decisions should include researching what kind of return the investment probably will make and the amount of risk that you will need to take (among many other criteria). In other words, the nature of investing is not so much about perception but more about the reality of the whole situation. After deep analysis of an investment, does your research concur with its marketed expected return?

Principle 108

Never invest more than you can afford to lose.

It makes no sense to risk losing what you need for the possibility of gaining what you want. If you need money to pay the essential bills, it would be foolish to use that money for investment purposes. I don't subscribe to the theory offered by many financial advisors of "pay yourself" first. This theory says you should take money from your income to invest before you do anything. This theory confuses priorities. It is more sensible to "pay your essentials" first and then invest. What good is it to be investing money when your electricity is out and you don't have sufficient food? Also, what will happen if your investment goes bad and needed money is no longer there?

This principle works even at a higher level of finance. For example, in the 1990s a company called Long-Term Capital Management showed how investors who were already wealthy were willing to risk everything they had just to make a little more. This company ended up with a catastrophic loss that jeopardized the livelihood of its owners and the stability of the entire American marketplace.

Principle 109

Gambling and investing are not the same thing.

"Although various marketplaces may appear to be games of chance at times, make no mistake, they are not the same. A market is a place for conducting business. Business is not a game. Games are for people to play and business is for people to work. A gambler bets and an investor invests, and the two are as different as night and day" (Criniti, *The Necessity of Finance*, 134).

Principle 110

Never gamble more than you can afford to lose.

Gambling addiction is a disease that can lead to permanent financial disaster. If you like to gamble on occasion, then make sure that you can afford to lose the maximum amount that you plan on playing. When you reach your maximum loss limit, then you must stop. For example, if you go to a casino and have $100 allocated toward your gambling fund, then you should stop playing when that money is gone. If you allow yourself to gamble more than your limits, then you subject your wealth to unnecessary risks and you may provide the key needed to unlock your potentially hidden uncontrollable gambling spirits.

Principle 111

*If you want to be a serious financial player,
eventually you will have to make a move.*

Only in rare situations can you create big wealth by standing still and relying on money to find you (i.e., hitting the lottery). Generally, either you or your money must be working hard to make more wealth. Investing is a method to help in the creation of large wealth by allowing your capital to labor for you. That is, you can use your saved capital to purchase investments that can help maximize your wealth. If you choose good investments, then your wealth can grow faster and vice versa. However, by sitting on the sidelines and not investing, you do not utilize the power of interest that money offers. Money talks and pipe dreams rarely materialize. If you're serious about really maximizing your wealth, then eventually you must put your money where your mouth is.

Principle 112

*Adversity can have hidden opportunities for
more wealth.*

When something bad happens, most people panic and are overcome with the glass-is-half empty-syndrome. The intelligent investor is always prepared to capitalize on negative situations. As the ancient Chinese proverb states, "When the dragon enters the parade, make it part of the procession." You may not be able to control what happened, but with deep reflection on the new situation, you may be able to control what could happen.

Principle 113

View every situation for what it is and not for what you want it to be.

You should strive to always be a realistic investor. Many unsuccessful investors will spend their whole life chasing investments that were built on personal fantasy. Every investment and its future performance should be assessed by its real intrinsic value not its imaginary value.

Also, if you have a losing investment, then accepting this fact is progress. It takes an advanced level of financial control to admit when one is wrong and face up to the real situation. This may hurt your ego, but it will help your wealth in the long run. You will then be able to discard these losers sooner in order to reallocate your capital to more productive investments.

Principle 114

Those who invest badly and run away, live to invest another day.

In other words, know when to cut your losses. Selling losing investments (without any acceptable chance of recovery) before the situation gets worse is money made. By keeping money that you could have lost, you are allowed to retain your wealth. It is better only to lose some money than all of your money. Always follow up on your investments to ensure that you cut your losses when needed. The longer you wait to sell a losing investment, then the higher the bill will be later.

Principle 115

Your wealth is only as strong as your last investment.

Consistency in selecting good investments is crucial to long-term survival. The efforts of wisely selecting a million great investments can be eliminated with one foolish investment decision. There are many well-established businesses that went bankrupt due to one bad investment decision of their last chief executive officer. How do companies that have been in business for 150 years go bankrupt? The same way that careless, greedy, rich investors do. They may jeopardize everything they built maybe just to earn a little extra return on their last investment.

Principle 116

Location is only one part of any real estate investment decision.

The old saying "location, location, location" is often taken out of proportion. Make no mistake; location is important in real estate. However, a great real estate investment decision should not be based solely off location but on many other factors, including its overall total marketing strategy, return, and risk. In the words of the legendary real estate investor Donald Trump, "First of all, you don't necessarily need the best location. What you need is the best deal" (Trump, *Trump: The Art of the Deal*, 54-55).

Principle 117

*The market price is only one part of
any investment decision.*

This principle was created to address all investments; however, it is particularly well suited for stocks. When you purchase a share of stock, then you become an owner of a business and you have voted that you believe in its financial potential. Stock investors should focus not only on the current price of stocks but on the present and future financial health of the companies they own. The market price, although important, may not always align with reality. It is important to focus more on the reasons why you want to invest your money to become the owner of any corporation. The most successful investors in the stock market, including Benjamin Graham, Warren Buffett, and Peter Lynch, have always understood this principle and have profited immensely.

Principle 118

It matters more how an investor uses funding than what source it is derived from.

Investors can obtain money to invest from many sources including the equity market, various types of loans, or their own retained earnings. Every source comes with different costs of capital, pros and cons, and risks. Although the source and its costs are extremely important to every investment decision, it is not as important as what the investor will do with the money. There may be justifiable situations where an investor should obtain funding with extraordinary costs (assuming there were no alternative low-cost options), for example, 20 to 50 percent. If an investment can earn returns greater than the cost of capital at a tolerable risk level, then it should at least be considered among the alternatives.

Principle 119

Guarantees do not exist in investing.

This principle can apply to many areas of investing. First, as the popular investment disclaimer states, "past results are no guarantee of future performance." In other words, historical returns earned from any type of investment can never give you 100 percent comfort that it will reoccur continuously (although it may in academic textbooks). If a stock earned 50 percent for one hundred years in a row, the year that you invest may upset the record.

Second, there are no guarantees that any technique for selecting investments will continuously work. Certain tools may work some or even most of the time, but there will always be that exception to the rule. Furthermore, as a successful technique becomes learned by the masses, the value of the technique may decline. If everyone knew how to pick great stocks, then great potential returns may become significantly impaired.

Principle 120

*Short-term above-average or below-average
returns on investments generally regress to
the mean in the long term.*

It is very difficult to beat the market, regardless of what investment market we are talking about. This is because it is the business of successful investors to find out if other more successful investors exist and the reason why they are successful. If they determine that these other investors have the right strategy, then they will usually vote to invest similarly. This psychological cycle causes large returns earned by a few to be spread out among a growing bandwagon of investors and thereafter regressing it to a mean. As mutual fund guru John Bogle puts it, "for all types of assets, the concept of regression to the mean is fundamental to understanding the financial markets" (Bogle, *Bogle on Mutual Funds*, 20).

Principle 121

Any investment tip should be well researched before being acted on.

It is tempting to act impulsively on investment tips, particularly stock tips. The allure may be derived from the possibility of earning great wealth on privileged knowledge that has not been processed by the masses yet. However, unsubstantiated tips can be dangerous. For example, stock tips have been a major reason for the loss of wealth of the average investor throughout the stock market's history.

Principle 122

If average investors could make money without any effort, then they would.

The hard work involved in continuous successful investing is often understated. Unfortunately, many people invest their hard-earned money into investments selected from the "easy way out method." That is, they may have selected an investment by a tip from a friend or the local news, by random selection without any research, by the weather forecast, or any other way that requires as little amount of their energy as possible to make a decision. As contrarian Humphrey B. Neill puts it, "The average investor does not think and does not wish to think" (Neill, *The Art of Contrary Thinking*, 51). This knowledge is powerful to real investors. The extra time that they spend researching an investment may profit from the mistakes of the many investors who didn't care enough to do the same.

Principle 123

Rebalancing your investment portfolio on a timely basis ensures alignment with your goals.

A portfolio is a collection of your investments at any point in time. Its value is constantly fluctuating as gains or losses are made. Without any monitoring of the situation, a portfolio can shift quickly to become inconsistent with your risk-tolerance level. For example, let's assume that you invested 100 percent of your money in a portfolio consisting of both 50 percent stocks and 50 percent bonds. If your stock investment performs very well relative to your bonds, you may end up with 95 percent of your portfolio in stocks. This may certainly be more than your risk tolerance allows (assuming that you agree that stocks are riskier than bonds). Thus, you may need to rebalance everything by selling stock to return to your risk-tolerance level.

Principle 124

Something is always perfectly visible in hindsight.

It is easier for an investor to say that he or she knew an investment was bad or good after the fact. However, the reality is that what really counts is what was already done. If you really knew what an investment was going to do (assuming you had the money to invest), then the outcome is the best proof. There is no point regretting about what you could have done because "you knew it all along." It is a better allocation of your time to prepare for successfully selecting your next investment.

Principle 125

Investment markets may be right most of the time
but certainly not all of the time.

This principle is usually unquestioned with most investment markets. However, when it applies to the stock market, this topic is highly debated. Yet, the majority of both sides of the efficient market theory are starting (after many decades) to agree that at minimum, markets are at least right most of the time. The debate lingers around the "all of the time" part. If the market has the slightest chance of being wrong some of the time, then there admits opportunity for above-market investment returns by some investors. Investment legends like Buffett and Lynch have kept this part of the debate an open case. Even Burton Malkiel, a major advocate of the random walk theory, states, "Markets are not always or even usually correct. But NO ONE PERSON OR INSTITUTION CONSISTENTLY KNOWS MORE THAN THE MARKET" (Malkiel, *A Random Walk Down Wall Street*, 106).

Principle 126

"Investments are like fruit; they need to ripen
before you can enjoy their benefits."
(Criniti, *The Necessity of Finance*, 143)

Every investment has a unique amount of time that it takes to become ready to show a return (if ever). There are some investments that are very short-term, like CDs and short-term bonds. They ripen quickly. Then there are many long-term investments that may take decades or more to pay their reward for holding on to it, like real estate or stocks. Generally, those investments that take the longest to ripen, pay out (or lose) the most.

Marketing

Principle 127

---

*Ultimately, profitability is determined by your
ability to persuade your customers of the
significance of your product or service to them.*

Marketing is a crucial subscience of economics and finance that needs to be considered by an economic or a financial entity. For example, a business may have a great product or service to offer. Yet, if people are not made aware of it or its benefits, then much effort may have been wasted. It is the responsibility of the business to be proactive in demonstrating to the public why they should spend their income on buying its goods or services.

Money

Principle 128

Civilizations that use money require it for survival.

In modern civilizations, money is a necessary tool to exist. The more money and total wealth that you have, the higher your odds are of having increased self-preservation, especially in critical times. Without money, unless someone else is paying for you to live (a process called *financial survival by a third party*), you will not meet basic needs such as clothing, drink, food, and shelter. Those who refuse to admit the importance of money will create their own impediment to successfully navigating through the complexities of our society.

Principle 129

Money does not cure all of life's problems.

With or without money, life is still a struggle. The sooner this lesson is learned, the faster one will approach life more realistically.

Although money is essential, it still has its limitations. The labor that you can buy with money can accomplish amazing tasks. However, the power of money is limited by the current abilities of technology and the knowledge of the existing labor force. For example, you can build skyscrapers or supersonic jets if you have enough money, assuming the technology is in place and laborers who know how to use it. Yet, before this technology was created and the laborers of this technology were trained, this option didn't exist for the wealthy.

This same argument can be applied to virtually every problem we can think of. If you have a headache, you may be able to buy a pill or pay a doctor to fix it. But there are still many problems that money cannot fix *yet*. Some examples include broken hearts, dead loved ones, psychological issues, rare diseases, and ruined relationships.

Principle 130

Money does not guarantee happiness, but it may provide better options.

Despite the enduring misconception, money does not guarantee happiness. Unfortunately, many poor people think that hitting the lottery will solve all of their problems, but as stated in the prior principle, it does not. Those who eventually become wealthy learn the hard way that many forms of unhappiness still exist even when you are wealthy. **Life is an up-and-down road, whether it is paved with dirt or gold.**

Money may not come with a lifetime happiness guarantee, but it does give alternatives to people that did not exist when they were poorer. For example, by paying off all debt, you can eliminate all of the financial stress associated with the continuous fight to make periodic payments. Also, money may be able to buy you better medical options, cleaner water, healthier food, and safer and stronger housing, etc.

Principle 131

Money can't buy you long-lasting love and respect.

Although this principle may overlap with some others, it is important to emphasize it by making it separate. There appears to be an almost endless number of products or services that one can buy with money. However, love and respect are at the top of the list of rare items that money can't buy. Well, debatably, you may be able to buy them temporarily, such as via prostitution or unconditional gifting. But in the long run, these two feelings must be earned the old-fashioned way, through your own efforts. Your time must be spent continuously demonstrating to other people that you deserve to be loved or respected.

Principle 132

Money is only a part of wealth.

Money is an asset that can help you buy products or services. But there are other aspects of your wealth that are also important to consider, for example, businesses, debts, equity, intangible assets, investments, moral assets, and spiritual assets. By only focusing on building your cash assets, you may neglect to assess your real comprehensive financial health.

Principle 133

The belief in what money can do is what makes it powerful.

Money is a tool of commerce used to make everyday labor transactions easier and to store wealth. Money can be tangible (e.g., a coin or a rock) or intangible (e.g., digital money or memory). Whatever currency is chosen, it must be remembered that money is just a symbol.

Many governments try to manipulate the quantity of money to have certain effects on the actions of its people. Yet, the reality is that it is the quality of money that makes it most effective. Once the users of money lose faith in its purchasing power, then the entire currency may be replaced by another.

Principle 134

*As the population increases, the benefits of money
and its accounting increase.*

On a one-person island, there is no need for money, although debatably there is a need for other forms of wealth, for example, the human skill to survive independently (this can be considered an asset). If you add a small family to this scenario, money is still almost unnecessary. Furthermore, in a very small town, money has limited advantages. Here you will often find much bartering and mental accounting. However, as civilization progresses, the big city adds layers of complexity to conducting business and storing wealth that only money and formal accounting could resolve. If our population continues to increase, as reflected by the growth of many megacities, then money will continue to gain significance to make the exchange of everyday labor easier.

Principle 135

Money is not the root of all evil and good.

Money by itself is not a bad thing, as it is often labeled. It is just a tool to exchange goods and services and store wealth. Its invention has helped many people live a much more comfortable life than our primitive ancestors. Money represents people's intentions, usually as one vote per unit. If you intend to have a nuclear bomb to blow up the world, assuming you find a supplier, you can use your money to buy it. However, if you want to help a good cause, such as feeding the poor, the money you spend will count as your vote for that cause. **Thus, the real root of most evil and good is the economic or financial entities that control the money.**

"Money itself, whether in the form of gold or paper, does not have a human conscience to decipher right from wrong. It is the person, group, organization, or nation that controls the money that has the ability to perform acts of evil or good by choosing to consume unethical products or services, donate to unethical causes, or pursue unethical investments" (Criniti, *The Necessity of Finance*, 186-187).

Principle 136

The history of money explains almost everything in history.

From inventions to wars, money has played a significant part in most aspects of modern human civilizations in the past and present, and it will continue to do so in the future. **People will live and die for money because its symbol is tangled in the beliefs of who we are and where we want to be, individually and collectively.** This principle emphasizes the importance of studying economics and finance in order to better understand the dynamics of money.

Principle 137

Money can only travel in space over time as fast as allowable by the form that it is in.

Money is the best realistic shape shifter known to humans. It can change into various forms, from digital to gold to paper and back. The closest other known thing that can do this is light. Light can cause you to see an image by shaping into the outline of it. But only money can change into an object completely in form, not just its outline.

It is this special characteristic of money that must be considered when analyzing its storage and transportation aspects. For example, imagine carrying enough money for a week's worth of groceries when it is in the form of the smallest coins available in your currency. A little heavy, yes? It would be a little lighter in the form of paper and even lighter if it was digital.

Large amounts of money in its heaviest forms, for example gold or silver, may need to be transported long distances by various larger means of transportation like boats, planes, and trucks. It costs a lot of money to store and transport these forms. However, in its lightest forms, for example digital, money is stored and transported by more efficient methods that cost very little or nothing.

Many physicists say that light is one of the fastest objects that moves in space, and they reference everything to its speed. If we find a way to make money take its form, then it can *also* move at the speed of light.

Principle 138

Never underestimate the speed at which a quantity of money can grow.

This principle operates under the academic concept of time value of money. The speed at which money can grow demonstrates its unique qualities. That is, through the usage of growth rates, whether using compounding or discounting methods, a pile of money can grow or shrink at various speeds.

Also, despite the misconception, it is not hard to spend large amounts of money quickly. If given unrestricted freedom, money can deplete faster than its owner can realize the severity of the situation. Large fortunes can be lost by careless monetary decisions in a year, a month, or even an instant (for example, money spent on bad investments).

Units of money can also be created very quickly for an owner. This may occur through the process of compounding, which entails interest earning interest. The more money that is compounded, then the more money that is created over time. At a tipping point, in just a small compounding cycle, a certain interest rate mixed with a certain currency amount can create unfathomable amounts of money. Of course this amount may be much larger than all of the money in the world, thus unrealistic. However, the fact that piles of money can become so large so fast illustrates why studying time value of money is so important.

Principle 139

*The value of money cannot be calculated backward
or forward in time simultaneously.*

To review from *The Necessity of Finance,* "a law of money motion is: when money is going in one direction at a specific moment, it must stay going in that direction" (Criniti, *The Necessity of Finance*, 170). For example, if you compound the present value of certain amounts of money for a period of time at an interest rate, then you will reach a future value. To reverse this process would be a totally separate calculation and process of money motion. This principle is essential to understanding how time value of money problems work.

Principle 140

Money, and knowing how to use it, consistently makes money.

Contrary to the old proverb, money alone does not make money, at least consistently; it also depends on the understanding and application of financial principles by its owner. This is what many ex-rich people didn't understand. Money can make money temporarily, but if it is foolishly put in the wrong place, it can vanish. The life cycle of the wealth of an individual is dependent on its use. If properly managed, a small amount of money can grow into a fortune quickly, and vice versa.

Principle 141

It is important to master making quick change of your currency.

The skill of converting one's money into larger or smaller units quickly can lend many opportunities to creating wealth or avoid losing it. This principle is particularly good when negotiating. If you can think monetarily faster than the party that you are negotiating with, then you may be able to know exactly what your next offer or counteroffer will be while the other party is still thinking. Having an advantage on a split-second decision process can positively affect every price mentioned, including the last one.

This principle can also help you avoid losing wealth. If you can calculate your change quickly, then you can determine if you were given the right amount of money or shortchanged (and possibly defrauded). In either case, you will be able to make an immediate reaction to address the situation before it is too late. For example, if you were given the wrong change by the seller of merchandise, it is easier to rectify the situation as soon as the change is given than to wait until it is much harder to prove (especially when dealing in cash).

Principle 142

A forecast of potential money is always less valuable than the possession of the real thing.

This principle is a derivative of the old saying "a bird in hand is worth more than two in a bush." Imagining being rich can be fun to do, but it doesn't help to pay the bills. Unless you really have money (or other forms of wealth), you cannot fully enjoy its benefits. Even with a great financial plan in place, external forces always have a chance of creating obstacles to obtaining income that appeared to be a sure thing. For example, you may never get that great job that was promised, or your "high quality" stock may stop paying dividends that you counted on. Any forecast, for example of the weather, means little if it conflicts with the reality of the situation. What good is a forecast of all sunny days on your vacation if the result was rain the whole time?

Principle 143

By always carrying some money, you are better prepared for the unexpected.

There are people who refuse to carry money with them. Some prefer just to have a credit card, but never cash. Some prefer to carry nothing. They may have many reasons for doing this, such as being afraid of losing it or getting robbed. However, it is better to have at least some pocket money just in case you need it.

What about emergencies? What if your car breaks down and you need taxi or bus fare? What if you become dehydrated and need something to drink? Without money to cover basic "what if" situations, you put yourself at risk of not being prepared for unforeseen circumstances. Ideally, you may want to carry just enough for basic needs, but not enough to attract the thieves.

Principle 144

*It is important to never carry too much money at
one time, unless absolutely necessary.*

This principle is interconnected with the previous one. Yes, it is important to carry some money with you at all times, but not too much. When you carry more money than is essential, then you take the chance that many bad things will happen. In particular, especially if the money is advertised, you risk having it stolen and being assaulted. Thieves seek out people who carry excess cash.

It makes more sense to spread the risk by only carrying enough money that you will need for a short period of time. I recommend enough for about one to two weeks. The rest of your cash should be placed somewhere safer like a bank or a vault. Of course there may be times that you need to carry large amounts of money for various reasons. But it is wise to limit these events to as few as possible.

Principle 145

It is important to always have an emergency fund of cash and gold.

There is an unlimited number of emergency situations that can happen to anyone at any moment. Although it is hard to predict what that situation may be, it is not hard to predict that money will play some role in it. The common solution to this potential problem is to create what is called an *emergency reserve* (or *fund*). Many financial planners over the years have recommended having a reserve that will usually cover at least three to twelve months of living expenses. Although this is a good start, I think that it could be a little stronger. To do this, I recommend placing at least six months of current living expenses in cash equivalents (e.g., a checking account in a bank), three months in actual cash stored somewhere fire-proof and safe, and three months in gold (this may need to be readjusted frequently to match the gold market price).

I have added extra layers of protection to the emergency fund for several reasons. First, contrary to what is believed, it is not always easy to pull out large amounts of money from your bank account at one time as modern local banks usually only keep limited amounts of cash in their vaults. You may have to wait for cash to be sent to your bank, which may take several days to weeks. Having some real cash on hand can tackle immediate needs.

Also, I have added the extra layer of protection requiring gold in an emergency fund for unique rare situations. Over the past several thousand years, money has taken many forms, ranging from paper to stones. Yet, the one form that has stored more value for the longest period of time is gold. You may not be able to completely trust that your current national currency will be around during your whole lifetime. However, the historical records of money demonstrate that gold may always be the standard that all monetary forms may be measured against and eventually replaced with in emergency currency situations. If (and this may be a long shot) your currency is eliminated, having some gold may help you to deal with short-term needs (hopefully at least until a new currency is created).

Principle 146

Nobody cares more about your money than you.

This principle has been observed in various forms by many great economists, from Adam Smith to Milton Friedman. There are some situations, such as a fiduciary relationship, where economic or financial entities would place someone else's monetary goals before theirs. However, this act works better in theory than in practice. Due to instinctive survival needs, the agency problem is always present to some degree. Even your family members (I am mainly referring to the extended family) may have their own financial problems to worry about before they can even think about helping you. This principle highlights the important conclusion that it is ultimately your responsibility to take at least some part (ideally complete control) in the management of your own money.

Principle 147

It is important to be extremely discreet about the quantity and the whereabouts of your money.

Only disclose financially related information to people you trust and only if you believe that they absolutely need to know. Bad, desperate people may kill for the value of a pair of shoes. For a little more, what they could do to you is limited only by their imagination.

Personal Finance

Education

Principle 148

---

*You don't need to become academically intelligent
to become wealthy.*

Higher levels of formal education are not for everybody. However, generally, you do need to know your trade better than the masses. A person who does the simplest tasks but can become more efficient than anyone else with that task will attract a profitable demand for her or his labor. Thus, a person who stuffs envelopes can become rich by stuffing envelopes better and faster than anyone else. The more knowledge you gain to improve the skills of your trade, then the higher the probability that your income will increase.

Principle 149

It is important not to waste your time and money on education that you won't need.

If you are absolutely positive that college is not for you then why go? Your money and time can be better directed in another path that will make you happy. If you want a career that doesn't need a degree, then why get it? If there are cheaper alternatives to learning more about your line of work, then these options should be considered. Some occupations don't require the level of knowledge assumed to come with an expensive diploma.

Also, lifetime students should strongly consider this principle. They may spend most of their life in school before getting out into the real world to make money. If your money and time spent on education are not justified by your potential future income, then you may want to reexamine your academic and career plans.

Principle 150

Spend more time researching for the biggest decisions of your life than for the smallest ones.

It is paradoxical that the average person spends an extraordinary amount of time researching the prices of smaller products and services that generally cost less than a week's pay but hardly an ounce of reflection for items that can majorly alter the dynamics of her or his entire wealth. For example, a person's search for the best prices of food, clothes, and appliances may consume more mental capacity than that devoted to researching the prices of a car or a house. It is important to get your priorities in order. If you spend an hour shopping for a good suit or dress at the best price, then maybe you should spend weeks or months shopping for a new house.

Principle 151

Never fully trust anything that you read in a financial self-help book without substantial research and/or confirming experience.

As finance is a science, there is a large amount of information that is considered fact. However, the art and theoretical part of finance is what leaves open a window of opportunity for misdirected advice. Many financial self-help books generally have a large amount of information that contains the author's opinion. There may be many other qualified financial experts that differ with her or his opinion on a particular financial subject.

There are many people who have invested and lost their fortunes on the general opinion of a self-help guru. This may have been avoided if they understood that what works best for one person may not work for everyone. General financial self-help books have information that applies to the masses but can be incorrect when applied to a specific financial entity. Also note that information is only as valid as its source. If the self-help "financial expert" has limited experience or knowledge of finance, then how can you trust her or him?

Principle 152

The experience of poverty can provide a lifetime of invaluable lessons.

The lessons of money and other forms of wealth are generally best understood more from a poor person who then becomes rich rather than a rich person who was never poor. The former generally learns the value of money best because he or she has experienced and emerged from the pain of poverty.

For those who have never been poor before, you should try it at least once (maybe in simulated form so you don't have to sacrifice your real wealth). It will build character. If you have been accustomed to wealth your whole life, an unforeseen bankruptcy may be equivalent to an inevitable extended death. It is better to be prepared so that you know what to do if poverty knocks.

This principle is best depicted in Edwin Lefevre's *Reminiscences of a Stock Operator* by his character who was based on the great stock operator Jesse Livermore. He stated, "There is nothing like losing all you have in the world for teaching you what not to do. And when you know what not to do in order not to lose money, you begin to learn what to do in order to win" (Lefevre, *Reminiscences of a Stock Operator*, 48).

Principle 153

It is easier for a poor person to adapt to being rich than a rich person to adapt to being poor.

Although having wealth does not solve all problems nor guarantee happiness, it still can make someone's life easier in many ways. With money, you can remove much of the stress associated with making ends meet. On the other hand, once you are rich, it is very difficult to adjust back to being poor. You will have to painfully experience a significant change in lifestyle and eliminate many comforts that you have become accustomed to.

This principle is best depicted in Edwin Lefevre's *Reminiscences of a Stock Operator* by his character who was based on the great stock operator Jesse Livermore. In real life, Livermore was famous for frequenting both sides of the wealth spectrum. He stated, "It does not take a reasonably young and normal man very long to lose the habit of being poor. It requires a little longer to forget that he used to be rich" (Lefevre, *Reminiscences of a Stock Operator*, 105).

Employment

Principle 154

It is important to choose the occupation that will make you happy.

A wise proverb says, "If you love what you do, then you will never have to work a day in your life." Money comes naturally when you do your work well. If you can love your work and do it well, then you can have the best of both worlds. Enjoying your lifetime work can be an invaluable intangible asset as it gives you priceless positive psychological rewards. Sometimes you may need to have any job just to make ends meet. However, ultimately you want to plan your life so that you can put yourself in a position to work because you enjoy it and not because it's required.

Principle 155

*It is important to choose an occupation that will
make you happy after many years of service.*

Most people choose jobs that appear to be very fulfilling at the time they start. However, eventually a learning curve may occur and be surpassed. If you learn all that you need to know and have reached a point of no more advancement, then you may become very bored. This may affect your finances and your health as it may be very painful to go to work every day to a job that you once loved but now don't. If you stay in an occupation for a long time, for many occupations, this process is almost inevitable. However, if you understand this principle and plan ahead, then you can minimize the pain when this time occurs.

For example, if you can find an occupation that allows your creativity to be incorporated into the job, then this minimizes the risk of your reaching complete boredom. In this case, there may always be an opportunity to express your originality into your work. Alternatively, many people may plan to enter multiple careers in their lifetime if their advancement and creativity potential peaks. They will retire from one career and join another at the absolute end of each learning curve.

Principle 156

It is important to choose the income path of least resistance.

There are indefinite ways of making money. One should consider the path that makes life the most enjoyable for her or him based on many factors. Particularly, find an occupation that is easiest to earn you money based off your individual talents, that makes you the happiest, and that has the most potential of maximizing your future earning power. For example, if given the choice between two identical jobs that differ only by stress level and responsibilities, it would be counterintuitive to choose the more complicated one that takes the most amount of time. Thus, it is in the best interest of an individual to choose the least stressful and most enjoyable occupation that caters to the individual's financial and psychological needs.

This rule also applies to supplemental income from investments. For example, if buying real estate has led you to earn more income with less effort than other options available with similar risk levels, then you should highly consider shifting more time to this income path. Real estate may not work well for everyone. However, it may be the easiest, least stressful method of maximizing income for those with a particular talent in this field.

Principle 157

Working in moderation should have a positive effect on your total lifetime earnings.

Try to avoid continuous excessive overworking for extra money. Too much overtime may increase your short-term wealth. However, in the long term, you may deplete your health and future earning power. This is because you may work yourself so hard that you may be physically incapable of working any more. Also, and more importantly, this behavior may lower the probability of you surviving to reap the rewards of your labor. To avoid burnout, follow the ancient Greeks' philosophy of doing things in moderation.

Principle 158

Occasionally spending money and time making yourself happy should lead to a healthier, more productive life.

When necessary, and within your means, sometimes it is appropriate to pamper yourself by spending money on things that make you happy. If you are happy, it may help you to think clearly, perform your work better, and to make more money. There are many people who work always and never spend. What is the point of laboring your whole life if you can never enjoy any of your money? Even if it is just once in a while, controlled spending for enjoyment purposes helps you to be mentally restored and focused on your personal financial goals.

Principle 159

It is important to only use state welfare funding when absolutely necessary and for as short a duration as possible.

If you live in extreme poverty where government welfare assistance is your only option to survive, you should create and implement a plan to minimize the amount of time as a dependent on this sort of funding. The sooner that you can free yourself from welfare and find alternative funds via your own labor, the faster you can live free on your own terms and pursue becoming financially independent. Welfare recipients generally feel trapped by the excessive rules to qualify for funds. The longer you stay on state funding, the harder it is to free yourself and your family from the dependency on the system (possibly for generations) and advancing in the societal ladder of wealth.

Principle 160

Working harder and smarter will help you to financially outperform the majority of laborers in any industry.

The combination of working harder and smarter will help you to become a part of the elite earners of any given industry. The logic to this is as follows. Most people (probably about 80 percent) are lazy and don't want to work a minute more than they have to. To test this, simply visit a large corporation and request for employee volunteers to perform an extra hour of unpaid work at the end of a work week. Chances are a large majority may not show. If you have the drive, you can outwork these people.

The majority of the rest of the laborers (probably about 15 to 20 percent) are usually working too hard to have enough time to think about the big picture. Most of this group can be outsmarted with the proper planning and training. If you can pass this hurdle, then you have made it to the highest performers of a given industry and should be able to command a higher salary.

Principle 161

You earn better when you feel and look better.

A better presentation may lead to more income regardless of what attire your business requires you to wear. Of course looking good is not the only factor, but it certainly helps. For example, you still have to carry yourself well enough to match your appearance. A positive state of mind and a feeling of confidence are often sensed by others.

Consistent proper appearance at your place of employment may lead to bonuses, more networking opportunities (it is hard to make friends if you smell bad), promotions, etc. There are also so many other indirect positive effects that you may have on the people that you will encounter on your job, including the boss and the customers. When people see that you take the time to cloth and groom yourself appropriately, then that sends a positive message about you while adding credibility to your character.

Principle 162

A master of a trade will generally out-earn an average laborer of many trades.

There are two old proverbs that have helped build the foundation to this principle. First, there is "a jack of all trades but a master of none." Another helpful proverb was recognized as far back as 1776 by Adam Smith in his *The Wealth of Nations*: "Jack of all trades will never be rich" (Smith, *The Wealth of Nations*, 669). The reality is that a jack of many or all trades *may* become rich, especially if he or she has good business skills.

Yet, assuming everything else is equal, a competitor who sells only one type of the same product or performs only one type of the same service will generally make more money. As illustrated by the concept of the *division of labor*, that entity will focus more time into becoming highly efficient at one thing than just average at many things. A trade's masters rightfully command higher premiums for their work than their "jacks of many" competitors as they can produce the best goods or services offered usually at a faster rate.

Estate Planning

Principle 163

You can't take your wealth with you when you die.

Unfortunately, there are many misers who do not get this simple principle. They go about their life maximizing wealth with greedy selfish desires to keep all and share none. It is these people who forget that when they die, their entire estate must be inherited by others, whether it is their heirs, a charity, the government, thieves, or their worst enemy. This process will occur whether they like it or not. Consider the Egyptian rulers who were buried with all of their belongings because they believed that they could take it to the next world. Many years after their death, various thieves found a way into the pyramids and took everything valuable.

It is actually counterproductive to be stingy with your wealth while you're alive because you still have a choice to give it away to whoever you want. When you're dead, then this option expires. Wealthy people also have the ability to help this world and its beings in some way. But those who choose not to help are despised by many for their selfish deeds. In the end, these people will be permanently remembered, but only for being self-centered cheapskates.

Principle 164

Inherited money is a reflection of the memories of a dead laborer.

When spending inherited money, consider the pain that the decedent went through to accumulate those funds. Essentially, someone's estate is mainly a representation of the final total of her or his accumulated labor and investments during a lifetime (ignoring gifts, other inherited money, winnings, etc.). Thus, it is a good representation of the net result of an individual's lifelong blood, sweat, and tears; joy; and pain and suffering. Armed with this new way of looking at an inheritance, a beneficiary is more likely to treat every unit of money spent with the utmost respect to ensure that it is not wasted away. **By preserving an inheritance, you are preserving the memories of its creator.**

Principle 165

The future plans of beneficiaries are not always consistent with those of the decedent.

It is important to incorporate the unexpected into any estate plan. Your estate plans may conflict with those whom you plan on giving your estate to. That is why it is important to be specific in your instructions about the people your wealth is allocated to when you pass away and how it should be divided.

Also, in regards to the welfare of your children (and/or other dependents) after your death, you can hope that they will take care of each other but plan otherwise. Siblings may have their own families to take care of and may be indifferent or incapable of caring for each other. Financial planners often encounter many situations where siblings may abandon each other in desperate times of need. If their parents were alive to see this, it may break their heart. Unfortunately, if this situation was not accounted for in the deceased's estate plan, then the weaker siblings may be left to struggle alone.

Family and Friends

Principle 166

Financial lessons in life need to be taught early for maximum benefit.

Prepare your children to learn the basics of finance from a young age. This may reap a variety of great dividends for the entire family when they are older. Children who are taught financial lessons are more prepared to manage their wealth as they mature. These same children may start to save and avoid dangerous financial habits early in life that may help them reach their financial goals at a younger age.

In addition, parents can profit from this principle too. For example, by raising financially intelligent children, they may be able to limit the cost of raising them (as opposed to a lifetime of raising financially dependent children). Some parents may even view this principle as a method of ensuring their own solid retirement, for example, by raising children who will be prosperous enough to take care of their aging parents.

Principle 167

The total cost to live for an individual is magnified for a family.

Many single people who plan to have a family may not account for the extra costs involved. It is important to remember that all of your expenses will now have to include the cost of every family member and her or his tastes for spending. For example, if your future wife has a big shopping habit, unless you can help keep her under control, you have just acquired her problem.

Also, note that if you plan a family budget correctly, although the aggregate cost has increased, the cost per person may have decreased. When you buy in larger quantities, you may receive discounts for various products or services. Also, you may now be able to share many expenses. For example, everyone living under the same household will share most food and utilities. Thus, they should have cheaper costs per person for these items compared to a single person.

Principle 168

Have only as many children as you can afford.

This principle could have saved many people from walking their entire life on the edge of the financial cliff. It sounds so simple, yet it is often ignored. Many people who can barely take care of themselves will procreate in the plenty. Some of them will choose to tough it out with several jobs for many years. Some may choose welfare (if available). Others will just walk away and abandon their families.

This principle also has economic value. In a free country that does not have a law on the maximum number of children a family can have, a person born in poverty with no income (or who plans to earn any) is allowed to have many offspring. Although the person cannot afford to take care of them, he or she may plan on welfare for permanent assistance. In the end, every citizen hurts from this behavior as it is each taxpayer that must cover the tab left over. The result is higher taxes and more poor welfare-dependent children who may continue this cycle until a horrible tipping point is reached.

Principle 169

A supportive life partner makes it easier to achieve your financial goals.

Most of the greatest business leaders had the support of a loving, loyal husband or wife, and they worked together to achieve their goals. Although love is very important, it is also important to consider the financial strengths and weaknesses of your potential spouse. I don't just mean the partner's current wealth status as that may change. More importantly, how good is the partner with managing money and other forms of wealth? Could he or she improve with just some training?

Together, a financially savvy couple can always find ways to improve their wealth. When life gets tough, it is important to have someone by your side who is able to help out and not exacerbate the problem. Choosing a spouse with bad financial habits, like gambling or being a spendthrift, and an indifference to saving for the future may create a downward, unrelenting financial spiral.

Principle 170

Supportive friends make it easier to achieve your financial goals.

Although money should never be the only consideration when choosing friends, it should be a consideration. Ignoring all nonmonetary ideal friendship qualities (like honesty and trust), good wealthier friends may help to create a more prosperous life than good poorer friends. The priceless connections made in the wealthier circles can help to secure a good long-term financial position.

On the other hand, good poorer friends who are ambitious and determined to improve their financial situation may also assist you in attaining prosperity. They may be helpful financial training partners on the road to financial independence. You may be able to learn financial lessons together while overcoming many obstacles to attaining wealth. Surviving many financial struggles with someone successfully can create a strong, lifetime bond between the two people.

Principle 171

Severed relationships can cost you the support of people who can be helpful in future situations.

Conflicts among various people that you have relationships with may happen at some point in time. Under the right circumstances, certain financial events can create a break between best friends. When these moments occur, it is important to keep a wider perspective of the situation. You may want to ask yourself, "Is there an alternative to what appears to be the chosen outcome?" Besides the fact that you may not want to sacrifice a good friendship, you never know if that person may be of value to you later on. As the old proverb goes, "be nice to everyone on the way up because you may need them on the way back down." A strong network of good relationships can be invaluable to you throughout your lifetime.

Principle 172

It is important to manage financial activities and discussions with family and good friends with the utmost care.

Very few people have learned the lessons in finance well. If you want to maintain good relations with loved ones, it is best to stay clear of any financial activities and conversations with certain people. To accomplish this, it is important to learn the financial limitations of every family member and friend (based on character, history, etc.) and use that as a measuring stick to determine what discussions and undertakings are appropriate and when.

Principle 173

Give children money and you feed them for a day, teach them to make money and you feed them for life.

This principle is derived from the ancient proverb that says, "Give a man a fish and you feed him for a day, teach him to fish and you feed him for life." The main lesson here applies to children also. It is an innate instinct for parents to want to protect their children in every way possible and give them a better life than what they had. Many people translate this instinct to giving their children whatever they want and whenever they want it. But don't buy into this mentality.

Although it has good intentions, this practice may lead to permanently dependent children who are incapable of caring for themselves. Giving to children in moderation is acceptable as it demonstrates your love to them. However, by excessively spoiling your children, you will deprive them of their opportunity to learn complete financial independence. In the end, you have done more harm to them than good.

Principle 174

Children who believe that they will not have to work hard for their money are more inclined to fail to meet their maximum potential talents.

When children believe that they will be given large amounts of wealth in their future, they are tempted to take the easy life. As long as the gifted money is still paying for their bills, the problem may not be as noticeable. However, trouble really starts when the donor stops giving or is dead. The money may run out because the children never learned how to manage it. Then they will be too broke, too financially uneducated, and/or too old to undo this mess. The final result is that you have done them a disservice and have caused the opposite effect that you intended.

Principle 175

*It is important to develop a core of people whom
you can trust with your life and your money.*

Strong relationships are one of those rare invaluable things in life. When you are absolutely sure that you have a family member or a friend who is capable of protecting your life and your wealth, it is important that you do everything that you possibly can to honor your part of the relationship. Friends will come and go in your life, but only the rare few will stay by you until the end. These are the keepers. They may come to your rescue in a variety of unique life circumstances and deserve your deepest respect.

Principle 176

---

*It is important to continuously test family and
friends for their loyalty to you and not your money.*

Although you may hope to never be betrayed by your own family
and/or friends, unfortunately, this part of life is out of your control.
Your best friends, brothers, sisters, etc. may decide at any point in
life that money is more important than you. This may conflict with
the core of who you are and break your heart if it happens. But
you must guard against it because, sadly, it happens very often.
**Because someone is born related to you doesn't automatically
guarantee that they will always honor, love, and respect you.
These qualities must always be earned, regardless of blood ties.**

Family and friends should be put through various tests (these
types of tests are beyond the scope of this book), particularly monetary, as often as you feel necessary. For example, you may feel
the need to put a new potential spouse through a series of tests, but
your brother maybe once every few years. This principle is especially important if you are already wealthy as you can significantly
reduce the probability of someone plotting for your wealth. Note
that people can change, so this testing must be a lifetime occurrence.

Principle 177

If a man cannot provide for his family,
then he may lose it.

A woman may leave a man if he cannot find ways to pay for the basic necessities of his family. A wealthy man may not need to work because he has his money to work for him. However, a poor man must work to pay bills. If a poor man does not want to work, cannot work, or cannot find alternative ways to make money, then he progressively increases the chance that his family will be redirected to another man who can. A woman can learn to live with many of a man's faults except for a husband who will not put serious effort into giving his family the security of a better life. Too many men are left alone for their failure to understand this principle.

Principle 178

Your financial security comes before a lover's beauty.

Avoid temptation to choose life partners, based on beauty alone, who are allowed to control your assets. You exist individually. If all of your assets are depleted, then you may need to start the wealth-accumulation process all over with time increasingly against you. This principle particularly applies to older rich individuals who attempt to be a "sugar daddy" or a "sugar mommy" to a younger lover.

Too many older wealthier individuals lose all of their wealth by being too trustworthy when taking on a much younger partner. The point is to exercise complete caution in these situations and understand the consequences of starting all over again at an older age. It is hard to predict the motives of a younger beautiful lover. Regardless, it is a safer proposition to ensure that you will be financially secure in any outcome of your relationship.

Principle 179

It is healthy for life partners to have a fair share in the financial responsibilities of a family.

Financially educate (and avoid excessively pampering) your life partner, especially your spouse, to avoid adding an extra burden to your children. There are many situations where the head of a household controls all aspects of money in a family. If this person passes away, the remaining spouse is left clueless as to how to survive. Thus, the surviving partner becomes incapable of doing anything on her or his own and may now depend solely on the children. However, at this point, their children may have their own families and problems. Adding a completely dependent parent to the child's daily routine may become a burden for many. The risk of this situation can be reduced significantly by proper financial instruction and planning, and by creating an environment where both spouses can contribute to the financial responsibilities of the family.

Principle 180

Anticipate that when you become wealthy, many people unjustly will feel a sense of entitlement to what you have earned.

Ironically, when you become rich, many long lost family, friends, and acquaintances magically reappear. For strange psychological reasons, they may feel that what you now have should be partly or entirely theirs. If given, these vultures will want more. If refused, they will behave in desperation to capture what they foolishly believe that they are entitled to. When that time comes, don't worry, as this process is inevitable. Tis' the nature of fools to claim what they do not deserve. Optimistically, wealth may make it much easier to see people's true character and allow you to judge accordingly.

Principle 181

Favors can be very valuable.

When you give favors, then you may get them back with dividends. By helping your friends prosper, you may indirectly prosper too. For example, if you refer business to a friend, eventually your friend may reciprocate when the opportunity arises. Don't expect immediate reciprocity as it may occur one day or one year later (or more).

If you instill this kind of behavior in you, then you may constantly and naturally find opportunities of all sorts for helping people succeed. The more opportunities you find to help others, the higher the probability that someone will try to help you. Thus, being helpful to others positions you for incoming opportunities.

Habits

Principle 182

Starting bad habits ends with bad financial consequences.

When you pick up bad habits, you may become like a dog endlessly chasing his tail. It is much wiser to reflect deeply on anything that is bad-habit-forming and the consequences it brings before choosing that path. For example, cigarette smoking addictions can lead to daily loss of health and wealth. A cigarette smoker who becomes desperate may pay extraordinary prices just for a puff. In the end, many financial goals may have been met sooner if these unnecessary addictions were never accumulated.

If your life already has many financially damaging bad habits, then eliminate them right away. You may never reach your fullest financial potential unless you break free the chains of all useless financial restrictions.

Principle 183

A tip is a reflection of the service that you perceived to have received.

It is important to tip well when necessary as it sends positive signals to the people who serviced you. Even if you are not wealthy, tipping well when appropriate tells someone that you care. A laborer is more likely to do a better job knowing that he or she is in the presence of a good tipper. If you like the service but do not leave a tip, then you may be labeled cheap and treated appropriately. However, if you don't like the service you received, then it is equally important to send that message via little or no tip. What you tip is also a form of feedback of how you want to be treated upon your next visit.

Principle 184

Sexual obsession leads to wealth depression.

Sexual energy when channeled properly can lead to greatness in all areas of life, especially in business. However, an obsession with sex or an inability to commit to your sexual partner may cost you decades of your life (or more) that could have been focused on building wealth. Many people spend an enormous amount of time focusing on sexual gratification instead of cultivating that same energy to more productive outlets. Napoleon Hill notes: "The desire for sexual expression is by far the strongest and most impelling of all the human emotions, and for this very reason this desire, when *harnessed and transmuted* into action, other than that of physical expression, may raise one to the status of a genius" (Hill, *Think and Grow Rich*, 276).

Principle 185

It is important to avoid impulse spending habits.

Think carefully before you buy anything. Every item that you buy requires proper reflection time on the benefits and costs of the transaction. Money spent easily may be difficult to replace. For expensive items, you should spend at least twenty-four hours to think about its impact on your wealth and at least one week to a month for items that are really expensive. Getting into good spending habits is one of the fastest ways to improve your wealth.

Principle 186

Bad social habits become riskier as your wealth increases.

Millionaires who have bad social habits stand to lose much more wealth than a person with nothing. It is important to deeply reflect on the consequences that these habits can have and stay clear of as many as possible. Once wealth is gone, it may never be replaced.

There are many direct and indirect ways to diminish wealth quickly from these habits. For example, a wealthy person who becomes addicted to alcohol or drugs may use every dime he or she has to feed that habit. Alternatively, a wealthy person may fall into financial trouble for directly or indirectly being associated with illegal activities.

Principle 187

Don't buy the bar if you can't afford a drink.

Don't make a bad habit of spending money wastefully on all of your friends, especially if you can't afford it. This habit temporarily multiplies your friends until your wealth is permanently divided. When all of your money is spent because of this foolish behavior, you will find out who your true friends are – probably the ones that are still around. You now would have paid for one of the most expensive ways of testing friendship. A true friend does not require you to support her or his lifestyle. A friend should want to help you to prosper and not leech onto and suck your money dry.

Principle 188

Don't buy the bar and expect your friends to pay for it.

It is not polite to give someone a gift but leave them with the bill. There are many situations where this may occur, but regardless, it always will leave a permanent negative reflection of your character on the other person(s). For example, if you offer to take someone out to dinner, always make sure that you have enough to cover the worst-case scenario on the tab. If not, when the night is over, then you may have one less friend.

Principle 189

You can't run away from yourself.

All of the tools in finance are helpless to people who can't admit and deal with their own major faults. These may include drugs, emotional problems, gambling, insatiability, and restlessness. **Until you know yourself truly and, with much courage, stand to confront your own weaknesses, then you may never be able to financially prosper to your maximum potential. No matter how fast or where you go, your problems will always follow.**

Principle 190

There is value in stability.

This lesson particularly applies to the nomadic types. Frequent temporary traveling can be very fun, whether it is for business or personal reasons. However, if you don't have the money to support this habit, then it can be a detriment to your long-term wealth.

Also, unnecessary permanent relocation can reduce or eliminate the prospects of financial independence, especially when it occurs at an older age. For example, a middle-aged man may move to the United States just because it appears to have many more opportunities. However, if this person had already built a career in his country, which entitled him to lifetime benefits if he stayed, he would have to sacrifice already secured income and start his wealth-accumulation process all over. Unless there is absolutely no choice but to relocate (for example, to escape war), then these types of decisions should be made early in life while the potential negative consequences may be smaller (especially if one has to relocate a family). Lost time may never be regained.

Principle 191

If you are a beggar or a thief only one time, then you may be labeled it for life.

There are many people who choose to enter the path of begging or stealing for various reasons (both moral and immoral). Once this path has been chosen, it may create many financial obstacles during one's lifetime. This is mainly because of the negative perception of these activities by society.

In particular, a history of stealing indicates that a person may not be trusted. Very few successful business-people want to do business with someone who carries a high probability of being dishonest. Of course people can change and become better, honest people. This doesn't change the reality that many people who are aware of a thief's prior history may automatically assume that the person is still a thief.

Principle 192

*Don't imitate your neighbor's buying behavior if
you can't afford it.*

Everyone has unique elements to their financial situation that dictate what items can be bought. It is not sensible to falsely pretend that your wealth is as great as or greater than someone else's. The whole idea of "keeping up with the Joneses" is very dangerous to the person with the smaller budget. Thus, it is important for you to be realistic with your monetary goals. Let your budget be your wealth compass.

Personal Assets

Principle 193

A fool and his wealth will eventually be separated.

A person who carelessly manages her or his wealth will ultimately have none. There are many examples throughout history where people have foolishly earned and spent their money without properly reflecting on the consequences of their decision. There is a misconception of a rich man as a person who will be permanently rich. A rich man who converts to "foolism" may not even have enough time to say farewell to the wealth he was once fortunate enough to have.

Principle 194

Ownership of vacation homes should be avoided unless you really can afford it.

Vacation property is a luxury asset that should only be purchased if your budget is big enough. There are many people who buy second homes without proper reflection on the future costs and difficulties of it. It is very difficult to personally manage a property that is not located within a short driving distance away. Thus, you may have to pay someone else to care for it.

Also, if you are using this property only a limited time a year, then you may want to consider other alternatives. For example, renting may be much easier and less costly for certain people. Contrary to what some "financial gurus" say, there are legitimate reasons for renting instead of buying property. Renting allows you more flexibility as to when and where you want to vacation without all of the headaches of owning.

Principle 195

Gift certificates and store credits should be used as soon as possible.

Holding gift certificates and store credits too long is risky for the customer. It is better to take your wealth now in these situations than risk losing it to various external circumstances, including company closures, company policy changes, and expiration dates. Also, it is important to consider the opportunity cost that you may incur if you could have invested the money used on store credits. For example, if you buy a $100 in credit to a department store but don't use it until ten months later, then you would have lost ten months of interest on that money. You could have just left that money in a short-term investment to earn interest while you waited until you needed to use it.

Principle 196

Many of the best things in life cost very little or nothing at all.

To maximize your wealth, you should identify what these things are to you (family, nature, etc.) and then spend your free time enjoying them. This will save you from spending money on other expensive activities that may never compare in quality. For example, on your day off you could take your family to a very expensive theme park. Alternatively, enjoying a day in a beautiful state-funded park with your family may only cost you the transportation to get there. If you walk there, it may cost you nothing.

Principle 197

It is possible to enjoy the luxuries of the rich on a modest salary.

If I may coin a word, a *poorionaire* is someone who can find creative ways to have the great luxuries of life on a poor person's salary without going into debt. In other words, there are ways to enjoy the same or similar things as the rich without spending a large amount of money. For example, if you like expensive clothing, then you can shop at flea markets or goodwill stores, etc., until you find what you like that is within your budget. Even if you settle for some rich people's hand-me-downs, their trash can now be your treasure. Also, you can travel to exotic places visited by the rich if you can shop for super discounts at the right time. The examples of this lesson are countless, but it is up to you to seek them out.

Principle 198

Products that live longer need to be replaced less.

Choosing products that will give you maximum durability can save you money in the long run. For example, if you are shopping for perishable goods like eggs, then choose the ones that have the maximum expiration date (for example, two to three weeks). There may be ones right next to them that expire in two days that you may choose for the same price. This would be a bad choice because you would be paying the same for something that will need to be replaced sooner. The problem may not be immediately noticeable. However, if you keep buying eggs (or any product) like this, over the course of a year or your lifetime, then you would have spent more money than necessary.

Principle 199

Large quantities of new wealth require acquiring financial knowledge before making any major decisions.

For those who have just received a large amount of money from an external source (for example, inheritance, lottery, etc.), you should take time to learn the essentials of finance before making any major financial decisions. This may take months to several years. However, at least when you are more prepared to deal with your new situation, the money will still be there. As the saying goes, "Money doesn't come with instructions." Fortunately, however, finance does come with lessons on managing wealth.

Particularly, many lottery winners become overnight spendthrifts and lose all of their money quickly. They may never have had or seen money in those quantities before. Because they didn't know what to do with it, they did what came naturally – they spent it.

Of course, if you have immediate needs to address, like credit card bills or mortgage payments, then this should be considered. However, purchases of large items, such as new mansions or jets, should be delayed until you can really understand the challenges that have been presented with the discovery of this new wealth. Some of the saddest financial stories are about people who acquired great wealth that was short-lived. Many times, these opportunities will never return to them, but their financial regrets may always linger.

Principle 200

Confidence in your abilities is an extremely important quality to acquiring and maintaining wealth.

Success starts from the inside. You need to believe that your specific talents will produce happiness for you and others. Wealth usually follows naturally from there. If you lack confidence in your work, then usually the result is inferior performance compared to your potential. Besides, if you don't believe in yourself, then who will? The greatest businessmen and businesswomen believed whole-heartedly in their talents and devoted all of their energy to prove it. The old cliché is true: "If you believe it, then you can do it."

Principle 201

The golden rule is those who have the gold make the rules.

This principle is interesting as it demonstrates a principle on rules, which provides a good example of the differences mentioned in the Terminology chapter. If you understand the golden rule (technically, it is a principle as defined in this book), then you will be enlightened on the way the real world operates. Unfortunately, there are many rich financial managers out there who could be better leaders for our planet and its beings. The impact of their financial decisions may have a butterfly effect that causes indirect negative consequences for many people.

The good news is that this principle is not as bad as it appears. All customers, both poor and rich, have the opportunity to pool their money to make the rules. When the majority of people (mainly in a free country) decide not to buy a particular product or service, then they have contributed to creating a rule against its existence.

Personal Finance Miscellaneous

Principle 202

When they miss, you are given an opportunity to let them pay.

This lesson is analogous to two fighters in the ring. If one fighter takes a shot and misses, then it is the other fighter's obligation to capitalize on this opportunity. When a good paying customer is a victim of a business's neglect of any sort, the customer should demand reciprocity (let them pay). Your money and time lost should be compensated to make you whole. Take advantage of these opportunities when they arise as they are an easy way to add value to your wealth. For example, if any of your utility companies makes an error that causes you to be without service for some time, then you should dispute this until you are compensated. Maybe they will offer you one month (or more) of free service depending on the situation.

Principle 203

It is important to complain as often as necessary when your wealth is at risk.

Any good paying customer has a right to be given the good service that he or she deserves. It is your responsibility to complain when you feel that your rights have been violated in any way (for example, unjust cable bills or taxes). Most people choose to be silent when other financial entities, particularly businesses, take advantage of them. Making money does require the courage to speak up when necessary. As the proverb states, "The squeaky wheel gets greased." The customers who complain the most (assuming their argument is valid) usually get prioritized in the business's "fires to die out first" list.

Principle 204

Silence, at the right moment, is golden.

Silence is not always golden, as the prior principle demonstrated, just when it is appropriate. There are many situations, for example in business negotiations, when keeping your mouth shut allows the other party to talk out their thoughts on the deal. By interjecting, you may be telegraphing your thought signals before the other party needs to know it, thus potentially negatively altering your desired outcome.

Furthermore, this lesson is especially important if you have a disadvantage in knowledge inventory compared to the other party. Speaking sends signals of what you do or what you do not know on a given subject. If you really believe that speaking will help your case, then do so. However, the hard part is admitting to yourself that your spoken word may not be helpful and then forcing yourself to be silent.

Principle 205

Don't win a battle if it may cost you the war.

This principle can be applied to various situations. Particularly, it is best to resist the temptation to earn or save a little more if it will cost you a lot. For example, let's pretend that a woman complained to her boss about the company's tuition reimbursement program not covering too much of the master's degree that she is pursuing. She may have argued very persuasively until the company paid for more of her tuition. However, six months later, the company decided to stop the program entirely because its higher costs were cutting into its profits. Although the employee's actions resulted in a temporary gain, in the long run her actions did more harm than good. This particular situation also reminds me of the old proverb "pigs get fat and hogs get slaughtered."

Principle 206

Being alive is expensive.

This is a lesson that many youth living at home at their parent's expense may not comprehend. Most of the cash-flow process that they may be familiar with includes money coming in from earnings (possibly from an allowance or side jobs) or going out for basic consumption of products and services. It is only when people start accumulating monthly bills that they feel the real pain of paying out for expenses.

Every person, poor or rich, needs money to live in our modern civilization. Bills must get paid regardless of how you get the funds. If you are not rich, then you will have to find ways to get money to survive. This lesson illustrates the necessity of studying finance to learn better ways to meet the goal of maximizing wealth.

Principle 207

Lend a little to get rid of people that are too much.

Give very small amounts of money to get rid of people whom you don't need around or who are taxing on your time, particularly, chronic beggars. Make sure that it is clear, though, that it is a loan and not a gift. A gift will bring them back, but a loan will only bring them back if they can pay you off. Generally, a chronic beggar who is given a loan will never come back.

Principle 208

If you live and/or operate in an environment of inflation, it can be a tool to help you accumulate wealth.

In general, inflation is not a good thing for the masses, but if you can use it to your advantage, then you may benefit. You can positively alter your wealth decision-making behavior when you leverage the knowledge that prices will probably go up. For example, you may want to work for an industry indexed for high inflation.

Alternatively, investing in real estate with a mortgage can be a good inflation hedge for several reasons. First, the market price of your house should follow general price inflation. Second, a mortgage is usually locked in based on a value that it constantly losing purchasing power. Third, inflation allows for higher rents.

Retirement

Principle 209

When you permanently retire, you may quickly expire.

Simply, you should never stop working (at least to some degree). This principle is based off the old-fashioned definition of retirement, where you may decide to stop working on a specific day (for example, at age sixty-five). The problem with that viewpoint is that it fails to consider that work in moderation is very healthy, especially if it is something that one loves to do. People who retire to do absolutely nothing for the rest of their life (especially after being so used to a lifetime of work) quickly find that they bore themselves to death (in many cases, my experience as a financial planner and retirement specialist has confirmed this literally). If you plan on not working in the traditional sense, at least plan to have a serious hobby to fill the natural desire of doing something productive with your time.

Retirement should be defined as working because you want to and not because you have to. With this new definition of retirement, anyone who loves her or his job, but is not forced to do it, is technically retired. If you reach an age where you are bored with your occupation and have the financial means, then you may want to consider switching occupations (even to a hobby that makes money). You may also want to reduce the number of hours you work when you are older. By choosing to still work but on your terms, generally, this results in a better proposition than the alternative. You will have more reasons to get up every day and feel proud of something. As a bonus, your extra income will allow you to keep up with any general inflation.

Principle 210

The younger you start saving, the younger you could retire.

All things being equal, assuming the same annual rate of return, present value, target annual investment payment, and target retirement amount, you will retire younger if you start saving at an earlier age. For example, consider a person who can earn a 10 percent compound return annually, has zero present value net worth, can invest $5,000 a year, and needs $1,000,000 to retire. It will take almost thirty-two years to reach this goal regardless of whether the person starts at eighteen or fifty years old.

Shopping

Principle 211

Being flexible with your purchase time can result in large discounts.

Many times it pays to go against the grain. When your shopping schedule is the opposite of the masses, you may find the best deals. For example, if you can vacation at a time of the week or the year that has less demand, then you will find significant savings. Another example may be buying summer clothes in the winter and vice versa. Fewer people demand these products at that time and the sellers still need to get rid of their inventory (many times even at a loss).

Principle 212

Lifetime guarantees become useless if the seller dies first.

Promoting lifetime guarantees for various products or services is an ancient marketing tactic. Many people easily buy into this promise without much contemplation on its validity. If a business gives you a lifetime guarantee and goes bust a few months later, then little was gained. When shopping for products or services that come with these guarantees, it is important to consider the actual probability of the company being around to honor its promise when you need it.

Principle 213

As long as buyers are ignorant of the truth, inferior products and services will continue to be sold.

There are many examples of products or services that are sold when equal or better quality, cheaper products exist. These examples range from overpriced low-quality building contractors to inferior mutual funds with high costs. If a rational person was given the option to buy a high-quality, less expensive product or a low-quality, more expensive product (assuming everything else is equal), what would the person choose? The better product for less, of course. Yet, opportunities to sell various inferior products and services will exist as long as information about them is not available or searched for. This principle emphasizes the need to always research before you buy anything.

Wealthy People

Principle 214

Being discreet and stealth, minimizes attacks on your health and wealth

Regardless of your wealth status, modesty is a rewarding characteristic. Rich people who flaunt their wealth not only may indirectly offend those who are less wealthy; they may also make themselves an obvious target to thieves. If you don't want to draw too much attention to your wealth, then devise a plan to keep a low profile. Some examples of being inconspicuous with your wealth include having a normal-sized house, keeping an average job, wearing jeans, etc.

Principle 215

The more you indulge in the luxuries of extreme wealth, the more you risk misunderstanding the reality of the masses.

Living life with too many luxuries may make one more disconnected with the general public (the common person), and often become resented. It is best for a person who has accumulated wealth to understand this difficulty and plan ahead. The person will eventually have to make an almost permanent decision as to walk among the people and share wealth (or give a perception of sharing, i.e., charity) or live a life alone in isolated extreme wealth.

By choosing isolation, the rich may also choose to struggle in a different way. Wealth is a social fabric that is connected at every seam. By living in isolation, a rich person neglects to contribute to the same force that has made her or his lifestyle possible. Even if you become very wealthy, it is important to never forget the struggles required to build your wealth. This knowledge will help to maintain compassion for the less fortunate who are currently struggling for a better life.

Planning

Principle 216

Failure to plan is a highly probable plan to fail.

Similar to the chance of hitting the mega lottery, there is a chance that you can succeed in maximizing your wealth without a plan. Yet, the odds are still significantly stacked against you. It is very important to set up a wealth-management plan as soon as possible, preferably before any major decisions are made. This plan must be flexible enough to make changes as needed.

Creating wealth is extremely difficult to do as there are so many different obstacles to overcome and lessons to be learned. If it is hard to do this with a plan, you can only imagine how hard it can be to accomplish this feat without one. As stated in *The Necessity of Finance*: "However, to reach one's goals without a plan would require an extraordinary, unlikely sequence of random events" (Criniti, *The Necessity of Finance*, 113).

Principle 217

When planning to manage your wealth, it is important to leave no stone unturned.

Ensure every aspect of your plan is covered by reviewing the details of all economic and/or financial data. For example, if you are still uncertain about acquiring a specific investment, it is generally best to wait until all of the information is gathered before making a decision. If you rush to invest and miss a small but important detail, like a liability that is not stated directly on a company's balance sheet, this can result in a large loss of wealth.

When it comes to making wise financial (or economic) decisions, you may only get one chance to do things right. Every one of these decisions should be considered as if it was the most important decision of your life – handled with the delicate care that a loving mother would take for her newborn. **One bad financial (or economic) decision may never be undone and can affect the way a financial (or economic) entity lives out the rest of its life.**

Saving

Principle 218

---

*Any money saved may provide you with an option
to spend it later.*

There are many famous quotes on savings throughout the centuries. First, Ben Franklin is thought to have said, "A penny saved is a penny earned" but actually said "A penny sav'd is Twopence clear, A Pin a day is a Groat a Year. Save & have. Every little makes a mickle" (Franklin, *Franklin: Autobiography, Poor Richard, and Later Writings*, 464). Similarly, the great economist Adam Smith said, "...as a penny saved is a penny got..." (Smith, *The Wealth of Nations*, 1112). In either case, this may not always be completely true. As investing is a part of saving, a bad investment may not always result in any addition to wealth. Actually, a bad investment can wipe out all of your savings and more (in cases where the owner has unlimited liability).

It is better to restate these quotes more accurately into a principle. Any money that you save *may* provide you with an option for future consumption. However, this largely depends on the amount of your savings available when you are ready to consume. In other words, it depends on your savings still being there when you need it and that there are no restrictions on its use (like restricted stock). For example, if you have hoarded cash that you stored under your bed before the house caught fire, then what good has it done for you when you need the money in the future. Or, if you invested that savings into a not-so-more-hot stock, then you may have nothing to show for later. In both cases, your many pennies saved are many pennies lost.

PART 3

CHAPTER 8

Conclusions

This book has taught us many things about the sciences of economics and finance through the form of principles. To understand why this book uses principles, we clarified some similar terms and explained how they fit into our overall analysis. *Natural laws*, or the laws of nature, are based on the same laws of the natural sciences and are inherent to all of the forces that act upon us. *Human-made laws* were created by humans to help us operate together in society. Similarly, *rules* are extremely subjective and can change with the opinion of the ruler.

A *lesson* was defined as some action or thing to learn. This book was about learning the most important lessons, in the form of principles, of economics and finance. *Principles* were defined as natural laws that are indicative to have enduring, highly probable value.

The principles in this book were derived after carefully considering all of the most important related subjects in economics and finance and their respective lessons. As they were designed to be scientific, they were required to meet six criteria in addition to passing my personal inspection based on experience. The criteria of each principle include: it should be time-tested; it should operate within the framework of economics and/or finance; it must be applicable to an economic and/or a financial entity; it should lead to wealth maximization for an economic and/or a financial entity; it should be highly valid (or accurate) and highly reliable (or consistent); and it should be a part of the top 1 percent of all economic and/or financial principles.

This book is the result of the most comprehensive investigation and compilation of the most important principles in economics and finance. Although there are many previous authors who have discussed wealth in various forms, both casually and scholarly, to my knowledge, there is no other work that attempts to scientifically capture the best lessons of wealth management throughout history in the way presented here. Some previous authors have noted important lessons, usually only a few, for various subcategories on the two sciences, for example mutual funds or real estate. Yet these lessons are only a fraction of the two sciences as a whole.

In the Literature Review chapter, I have provided a brief overview of some of the literature that is related to this topic. Although it is certainly not exhaustive, it provided a good starting point to understanding why this book's time has come. The principles of this book are a product of my research mainly from every major economic and financial work starting from Ben Franklin to the present. Furthermore, I have researched the most important business people throughout the past few centuries, including John D. Rockefeller and Warren Buffett, for some of their own personal lessons. From this research, I have found common themes, consistent with my own experiences in the field, which also have helped shape the principles listed in this book. Finally, any literature published prior to my *The Necessity of Finance* in 2013 was limited because the publications' authors were not fully able to investigate and discover true principles of wealth management without the proper paradigm presented in that book.

The principles of the book were created mainly from personal qualitative analysis by the author. In particular, they were created from my many years of field experience, including but not limited to my work as a finance professor, a financial planner, a financialist, and an investor. The principles were gathered from at least fifteen years of observations and note taking in the financial field. The original total potential principles list that was accumulated amounted to more than one thousand. However, this list was significantly reduced in order to meet the high standards of an ideal true principle defined earlier.

Many of the principles in this book were also derived from past qualitative as well as quantitative analysis done by other economists, financialists, and economic and financial managers, both directly and indirectly. Each principle was structured for future survey research and data analysis to eventually improve the limited quantitative analysis done directly by the author and to complement the qualitative field research already used, in addition to the possible use of other scientific methods, such as case studies or experiments, to increase the overall validity of these principles.

There are several limitations to consider from the material presented in this book. First, there are so many important lessons to learn from economics and finance that it was very difficult to determine specifically which ones are the most significant. Second, it is difficult to scientifically prove the validity of this book's principles in the absolute sense. Third, it is written by a financialist. Fourth, very little quantitative analysis was used by the author to form the principles in this book. Fifth, it is difficult to accurately calculate the probability of the principles listed here to be applicable within the designated arbitrary range of time of two thousand years minus or plus from the present. Sixth, this book is limited in that it is a human's attempt to capture natural laws in economics or finance. Seventh, each of the principles is analyzed very briefly. Eighth, these principles may overlap with each other in various degrees. Finally, this book is limited because it is not complete. That is, it is a work in progress.

It is hoped that you can consider the difficulties in writing a book of this magnitude in order to excuse the limitations listed above (and any others not mentioned). Unfortunately, limited resources, such as money, space, and time, impeded this current study from gathering more quantitative supporting data. Despite these limitations, this book teaches many better ways to manage wealth formed mainly from an often underappreciated qualitative methodology, which includes many years of a variety of experiences in the financial world. In addition, I have also spent many years researching many of the greatest minds in the fields of economics and finance to gather ideas for this book.

Finally, it is hoped that you will always treasure these most important lessons (in the form of principles) in two of the most important sciences to our planet. It is now possible to better learn these sciences of economics and finance through them. They will wait patiently at your door to help you combat your economic and financial struggles. They will wait patiently at your door to help you achieve your economic and financial goals. But only you can invite them in. Carpe diem!

Bibliography

This bibliography mainly lists works whose authors were specifically quoted. For all other authors and works not listed here, please see the Index.

Bogle, John C., *Bogle on Mutual Funds: New Perspectives for the Intelligent Investor* (McGraw-Hill, 1994).

Brennan, Jack, *Straight Talk on Investing: What You Need to Know* (Hoboken: John Wiley & Sons, Inc., 2002).

Carnegie, Dale, *How to Win Friends and Influence People* (New York: Simon & Schuster, 2009).

Clason, George S., *The Richest Man in Babylon* (New York: Signet, 1988).

Covey, Stephen R., *The 7 Habits of Highly Effective People* (New York: Free Press, 2004).

Criniti, Anthony M. IV, *The Necessity of Finance: An Overview of the Science of Management of Wealth for an Individual, a Group, or an Organization* (Philadelphia: Criniti Publishing, 2013).

Franklin, Benjamin, "An ounce of prevention is worth a pound of cure."

Franklin, Benjamin, *Franklin: Autobiography, Poor Richard, and Later Writings* (New York: The Library of America, 1997).

Getty, J. Paul, *How to Be Rich* (New York: Jove Books, 1983).

Hazlitt, Henry, *Economics in One Lesson* (New York: Three Rivers Press, 1979).

Hill, Napoleon, *Think and Grow Rich* (United Kingdom: Capstone Publishing Ltd, 2011).

Lefevre, Edwin, *Reminiscences of a Stock Operator* (Hoboken: John Wiley & Sons, Inc., 2006).

Malkiel, Burton G., *A Random Walk Down Wall Street: The Time-Tested Strategy for Successful Investing* (New York: W. W. Norton & Company, Inc., 2012).

Neill, Humphrey B., *The Art of Contrary Thinking* (6th ed.) (Caldwell: Caxton Press, 2010).

Ramsey, Dave, *Financial Peace Revisited* (New York: Viking Penguin, 2003).

Smith, Adam, *The Wealth of Nations* (Bantam Classic ed.) (New York: Bantam Dell, 2003).

Templeton, John Marks, *The Templeton Plan: 21 Steps to Personal Success and Real Happiness* (New York: HarperPaperbacks, 1992).

Templeton, John Marks, *Worldwide Laws of Life: 200 Eternal Spiritual Principles* (Radnor: Templeton Foundation Press, 1998).

Trump, Donald J., *Trump: The Art of the Deal* (New York: Ballantine Books, 2005).

Williams, John Burr, *The Theory of Investment Value* (Fraser Publishing Company, 1997).

Appendix A: Questionnaire Sample A

THIS SAMPLE IS USED TO DETERMINE THE RESPONDENT'S OVERALL OPINION OF THE VALIDITY (ACCURACY) OF EACH PRINCIPLE BELOW. IT IS USED FOR ILLUSTRATION PURPOSES ONLY FOR POTENTIAL FUTURE STUDIES. PLEASE NOTE THAT EACH RESPONDENT SHOULD READ *THE MOST IMPORTANT LESSONS IN ECONOMICS AND FINANCE* BY DR. ANTHONY M. CRINITI IV FIRST BEFORE CONTINUING TO REDUCE ANY AMBIGUITY.

Please circle the number corresponding to the rating number from the rating scale that best describes your opinion of the validity (accuracy) of the following principles. Please answer each question with a single response.

Rating Scale:

Strongly Agree	Agree	Neutral	Disagree	Strongly Disagree
5	4	3	2	1

Principle 1: It can take a lifetime to build a solid business and moments to destroy it.

    5   4   3   2   1

Principle 2: It is the owner's responsibility to ensure that her or his business survives, not the customer.

    5   4   3   2   1

Principle 3: Many singles may be better than one home run.

    5   4   3   2   1

Principle 4: Almost every idea can transform into a successful business if applied correctly.

    5   4   3   2   1

Principle 5: An army of many can't stop an idea whose time has come.

    5   4   3   2   1

Principle 6: Never let your competitors know what you're thinking before your ideas are publicized.

    5   4   3   2   1

Principle 7: When making more money than the competition because of a rare advantage, it is time to work harder than ever.

    5   4   3   2   1

Principle 8: Knowledge breeds wealth.

 5 4 3 2 1

Principle 9: If you have the option, eliminate the difficult clients for maximum efficiency.

 5 4 3 2 1

Principle 10: If you have the option, choose your customers based on their character and not their wallet size.

 5 4 3 2 1

Appendix B: Questionnaire Sample B

Please circle the number corresponding to the rating number from the rating scale that best describes your opinion on whether each of the following principles should be considered one of the most important lessons in economics and/or finance. Please answer each question with a single response.

269

Rating Scale:

Strongly Agree	Agree	Neutral	Disagree	Strongly Disagree
5	4	3	2	1

Principle 1: It can take a lifetime to build a solid business and moments to destroy it.

    5   4   3   2   1

Principle 2: It is the owner's responsibility to ensure that her or his business survives, not the customer.

    5   4   3   2   1

Principle 3: Many singles may be better than one home run.

    5   4   3   2   1

Principle 4: Almost every idea can transform into a successful business if applied correctly.

    5   4   3   2   1

Principle 5: An army of many can't stop an idea whose time has come.

    5   4   3   2   1

Principle 6: Never let your competitors know what you're thinking before your ideas are publicized.

5   4   3   2   1

Principle 7: When making more money than the competition because of a rare advantage, it is time to work harder than ever.

5   4   3   2   1

Principle 8: Knowledge breeds wealth.

5   4   3   2   1

Principle 9: If you have the option, eliminate the difficult clients for maximum efficiency.

5   4   3   2   1

Principle 10: If you have the option, choose your customers based on their character and not their wallet size.

5   4   3   2   1

Index

Made in the USA
Middletown, DE
13 August 2022

71321080R00166